MW00564451

THE MAYAN ASTROLOGY HANDBOOK

By
Abby Isadora Haydon
www.spiritualguidance.com

We Welcome you to the Evolution

This is your opportunity, To get tuned in,
To the Tzolkin, To join the harmony,
To heal our Mother, To join the galactic community,
As a warmly loved, And loving sister/brother

DEDICATION

This book is dedicated to Mayan astrology scholar Ian Xel Lungold 1949-2005. He was my friend, lover and teacher of Mayan astrology. It is my hope that this book will fulfill his dream of making Mayan astrology accessible to our modern world.

TABLE OF CONTENTS

INTRODUCTION

The knowledge in this book did not come into my life through a burning desire to learn about Mayan astrology. I learned Mayan astrology because I feel in love with Ian Xel Lungold and wanted to know all that interested him. Ian's constant focus and total dedication to Mayan astrology permeated my mind and emotions during the two years we lived and traveled together. In sharing his life and helping him manifest his goals, I learned his system of Mayan astrology. He took me to Mexico and Guatemala and introduced me to Mayan shamans and Day Keepers, who worked with the astrology calendar, the Tzolkin. He showed me how the system of Mayan astrology and its cycles within cycles worked. Ian and I were able to accomplish a great deal, in the world of Mayan astrology, before he passed in 2005. Ian created the charts that are in this book, that were sanctioned by the head of the Mayan Council of Elders of Guatemala. These charts took the complicated procedure of finding one's Mayan astrology day sign and distilled the necessary information into charts that make it easy and simple for you to find your Mayan astrology sign. Together we also started the web site www.mayanmajix.com. You can find out more about Ian Xel Lungold on this site. In the past 13 years, Mayan Majix.com has become a focal point for all things Mayan. The full story of my time with Ian is found in my first book, The Mayan Sacred Count of Days.

In the two years that we lived and traveled together, I came to grasp this simple yet profound system of knowledge. His shared with me his understanding of the personality of each day sign and the way the four directions or elements of fire of the East, water of the West, air from the North and earth for the South influence each other every day. This is really his knowledge and understanding. I am just documenting his work as I know it.

As I became familiar with the cycles of this astrological system, I realized that each new day had a relationship to my day sign and an effect upon my energy and life. Through Ian's guidance, I watched the days and took note of how the present day's direction/element affected my own direction/ element. I saw the result each day had on my activities and achievements. Ian told me that every four days I would have an empowering day, when the direction of the present day was the same as my direction. These days were good for business and accomplishment in the world. When the direction of the present day was challenging for me, my energy would not be as strong and I would not have my highest energy on those days. I also came to note that these days would resolve long standing conflicts or clear up problems. When the present day was supportive to me, I would feel nurtured as the energy of that day comforted me on many levels and I got help in many ways. On the days that Ian called mystery days; I could have a really good day, or a really difficult day. These days always brought the unexpected. Ian described these days as an opening to Great Mystery or the Unknown. He would say that these days allowed the hidden workings of the Universe to connect with us. He also said that on these days our positive or negative actions, (like the concept of Karma) would come back to me.

Ian and I did ceremony to welcome in the new Mayan week every 13 days. I saw how the ruler of each new Mayan week, as well as the ruler of each day, affected me. Each of the 20 weeks is ruled by a day sign and its direction. Weeks ruled by the South day signs are focused on the earth, the body and the material world. The fire sign weeks, bringing the power of the East, are full of energy and movement. The weeks ruled by the West, through the element of water, have the connection to the sub conscious, spirituality and artistic expression. When the ruler of the present Mayan week is from the North, the element of air takes over and brings communication and knowledge both new and ancient. Ian taught me to be mindful of how my day sign interacted with the ruler of the Mayan week. In challenge weeks, I did not press for big issues. Empowering weeks were the time to make strides in accomplishment. Nurturing weeks were good for handling relationship themes, and Mystery weeks always brought surprises to embrace.I hope that you have gotten the idea that following the cycles of the days and weeks can help you organize your time and energy so that it will be most effective.

What I call Western astrology, or the astrology that documents the impact of the planets in our solar system, is very useful in tracking long range influences of one to three years. Mayan astrology documents the impact of the energy from the center of the galaxy that hits us daily. The Maya feel that this is an important influence on us. I have found that when a person knows their Mayan astrology sign and its tendencies, they recognize aspects of their temperament that are not covered in Western astrology. The two systems together help us to understand the totality of our nature. This is the value of incorporating Mayan astrology in your life.

Mayan astrology can be related to Echart Tole and The Power of Now. The knowledge of the Maya shows us the nature of the present day and gives credence to the timeless book by Ram Das, Be Here Now. The Maya have given us the gift of how to greet the new day in the way that is best for each of us.

PREFACE

I feel it is important to share that this book is written from the perspective of an astrologer. I will be the first to admit that I do not have the connection to the Maya of today that many other writers on the subject do. I present this book as a system of astrology. The Mayan Astrology Handbook relates all of the basics of this astrological system.

My goal in writing this book has been to define the basics of this system as it may have been used at the time of ancient Mesoamerica. In doing a vast amount of research, I have found that even the Maya of today have made changes in this system. I feel that this discrepancy has developed due to the isolation that the Mayan civilization has experienced over the millenniums. Over time the tribes from different regions changed many aspects of the Tzolkin, or astrological calendar. The names of the day signs, the count of the calendar (which day it is according to different tribes) have all been subject to a lot of different definitions.

The ancient Maya had many calendars. The one with the end date of 12/21/2012 is called the Long Count calendar. It documents a 25,000 year cycle. I have also found that the contemporary Maya have blended these calendars. The Kiche' Maya have blended the solar calendar with the Tzolkin and have Monkey as their first day sign instead of Crocodile.

In Western astrology, the majority of astrologers agree about the traits of a Taurus or a Libra. In the world of Mayan astrology, there is no such agreement. Each tribe and their day keepers and elders have different opinions of the nature of each sign. What I have done is to define the personality of each day sign so that its basic nature is easy to understand. I have combined research, particularly that done by astrologer Bruce Scofield and the experience of contact with the Maya of today from Ian Xel Lungold. I have combined these two sources of information to define a system of Mayan astrology that is simple to incorporate into daily life. In working with many people, I have come to see that the definitions of the personalities of the day signs are very accurate. I have also found the compatibility factors between day signs to be very accurate.

My perspective on my rendition of the astrological system of the Maya is that it now is a complete cycle of experience. There are cycles every four days and every thirteen days. This book helps you understand how the directions of the Tzolkin, interact with each other. These cycles are smaller divisions of the many cycles that make up the Mayan concepts of time and rebirth.

My unique contribution to using Mayan astrology is my 3 step method of relating to Mayan astrology. My method of attuning to Mayan astrology will help people have an even closer connection to the Tzolkin, and the energy that each day brings from the Hu Nab ku. The first part will give you the basic information of your day sign, tone and the Mayan week of your birth. This is like knowing you are an Aires or a Gemini. If that is all you want to explore now, knowing that is good.

If you want to follow along with each day to be aware of how you can successfully interact with the energy from the galactic center, then you will be able to look up each day and see how to interact with it.

If you REALLY want to get involved, then do ceremony for each new Mayan week to welcome it in. This will bring even more understanding of the day signs and how they impact each week.

With this in mind, it is my hope that the reader will have a connection to Mayan astrology that they can use in their daily life.

THE TZOLKIN AND HOW IT WORKS

The Tzolkin, that is one of the few Mayan calendars that is still used, was adapted by the ancient Maya from the same basic astrological calendar used by the Olmec, Toltec and Aztec cultures. The large astrology stone the Aztecs made, that is found everywhere in Mexico, has the same basic astrology signs as the Mayan astrology calendar. Only the names of the astrology signs and some of the meanings were changed by the Maya.

The Tzolkin is still used today by the Maya in their villages in Southern Mexico, Guatemala, Belize and Honduras. The Mayans use this calendar to be aware of influences in their daily life and to know when to do ceremonies and other important activities. The personality of each child is clear to the Maya according to the day on which they are born. Their system of astrology helps them decide who will have what role in the life of the village culture.

The Tzolkin is a perpetual calendar. It continues to recycle every 260 days, or 9 months. The number of 260 is attained by multiplying the two numbers that are the foundation of the Mayan astrology system:13 and 20. Ian would bring up the fact that 260 days or nine months is the gestation time of the human embryo. Many Mayan scholars have related that 20 is the number of fingers and toes and that there are 13 major joints in the body.

The Mayan astrology sign has two basic components. It is comprised of one of 20 day lords or as they have come to be known, day signs. The day sign can be likened to the sun sign in Western astrology. The second part of your Mayan astrology sign is a number from one to thirteen. The combination of the 20 day signs and a number from 1 to 13 attached to each day sign combine to create 260 unique day sign/number personality combinations. The day sign and number equate to the sun and moon influences in Western astrology.

The basic nature of each of the 260 day sign/number combinations is also influenced by the Mayan week into which each person is born. The ruler of the Mayan week, that starts each new week with the number one, acts like a subtle watercolor wash over your personality. You are impacted by the influence of the day sign that rules the week of your Mayan birthday as well as your personal day sign and number.

For instance, if your Mayan birthday is 4 Jaguar, you will also be influenced by the Monkey day sign since you are born in a Monkey week. That may translate into an interesting duality for the 4 Jaguar people. The basic nature of the Jaguar is to stay out of the limelight. The 4 number makes the Jaguar want to stay within whatever they consider to be their foundation or home. However, the Monkey influence many create a desire within the 4 Jaguar person to come out of their lair a bit. The stimulation of the extremely social ruler of the Mayan week, Monkey, may bring the 4 Jaguar person out of their cave so that they will enjoy being the center of attention or where the action is. The 4 Jaguar person may embody other traits of the Monkey persona and might have a lot of creative talents. Even though this may sound a bit confusing, the Mayan astrology system is very simple and easy to follow. Think of Mayan astrology as making a sandwich. The bread is the day sign, the filling the number, but the mayo and mustard of the ruler of the Mayan birth week add a lot to the final taste of the sandwich.

These charts in this book were created by Ian Xel Lungold and are made available courtesy of www.mayanmajix.com

The first action that you should take is look up your birth year and day/month on the following charts. First you need to look up your year of birth on the following Year Chart.

Year Chart

YR	X	YR	X	YR	X	YR	X	YR	X	YR	X	YR	X	YR	X
1923	117	1936	186	1949	254	1962	62	1975	130	1988	199	2001	7	2014	75
1924	223	1937	31	1950	99	1963	167	1976	236	1989	44	2002	112	2015	180
1925	68	1938	136	1951	204	1964	13	1977	81	1990	149	2003	217	2016	26
1926	173	1939	241	1952	50	1965	118	1978	186	1991	254	2004	63	2017	131
1927	18	1940	87	1953	155	1966	223	1979	31	1992	100	2005	168	2018	236
1928	124	1941	192	1954	260	1967	68	1980	187	1993	205	2006	13	2019	81
1929	229	1942	37	1955	105	1968	174	1981	242	1994	50	2007	118	2020	187
1930	74	1943	142	1956	211	1969	19	1982	87	1995	155	2008	224	2021	32
1931	179	1944	248	1957	56	1970	124	1983	192	1996	1	2009	69	2022	137
1932	25	1945	93	1958	361	1971	229	1984	38	1997	106	2010	174	2023	242
1933	130	1946	198	1959	6	1972	75	1985	143	1998	211	2011	19	2024	88
1934	235	1947	43	1960	112	1973	180	1986	248	1999	56	2012	125	2025	193
1935	80	1948	149	1961	217	1974	25	1987	93	2000	162	2013	230	2026	38

Once you have found your year of birth, write down the number next to it on a paper or put it on a calculator.

Then look up your day and month of birth on the Month/Day Chart. Write down the number you get when your day and month of birth intersect.

Next you will add these two numbers together. If they add up to less than 260, you can just go find the third number you came up with on the Tzolkin chart. If the number you got from adding your year and month/day numbers together is more then 260, subtract 260 from the larger number, and that will be your Mayan birthday.

If you were born in January or February, like Ian and I were, then you use the year before your birth year on the Year chart. Ian was born in January of 1949 so he had to go to 1948 for his year number.

Day/Month Chart

Day	JAN	FEB	MAR	APR	MAY	JUN	JUL	AUG	SEP	OCT	NOV	DEC
1st	46	77	0	31	61	92	122	153	184	214	245	15
2nd	47	78	1	32	62	93	123	154	185	215	246	16
3rd	48	79	2	33	63	94	124	155	186	216	247	17
4th	49	80	3	34	64	95	125	156	187	217	248	18
5th	50	81	4	35	65	96	126	157	188	218	249	19
6th	51	82	5	36	66	97	127	158	189	219	250	20
7th	52	83	6	37	67	98	128	159	190	220	251	21
8th	53	84	7	38	68	99	129	160	191	221	252	22
9th	54	85	8	39	69	100	130	161	192	222	253	23
10th	55	86	9	40	70	101	131	162	193	223	254	24
11th	56	87	10	41	71	102	132	163	194	224	255	25
12th	57	88	11	42	72	103	133	164	195	225	256	26
13th	58	89	12	43	73	104	134	165	196	226	257	27
14th	59	90	13	44	74	105	135	166	197	227	258	28
15th	60	91	14	45	75	106	136	167	198	228	259	29
16th	61	92	15	46	76	107	137	168	199	229	260	30
17th	62	93	16	47	77	108	138	169	200	230	1	31
18th	63	94	17	48	78	109	139	170	201	231	2	32
19th	64	95	18	49	79	110	140	171	202	232	3	33
20th	65	96	19	50	80	111	141	172	203	233	4	34
21st	66	97	20	51	81	112	142	173	204	234	5	35
22nd	67	98	21	52	82	113	143	174	205	235	6	36
23rd	68	99	22	53	83	114	144	175	206	236	7	37
24th	69	100	23	54	84	115	145	176	207	237	8	38
25th	70	101	24	55	85	116	146	177	208	238	9	39
26th	71	102	25	56	86	117	147	178	209	239	10	40
27th	72	103	26	57	87	118	148	179	210	240	11	41
28th	73	104	27	58	88	119	149	180	211	241	12	42
29th	74	105	28	59	89	120	150	181	212	242	13	43
30th	75		29	60	90	121	151	182	213	243	14	44
31st	76		30		91		152	183		244		45

On the Tzolkin chart there are two numbers. The day or Kin number, from 1-260 is there to help you find your location on the chart. My Kin number is 118. Above that is the number from 1-13 which is your number within the Mayan week. Being that I am a One Flint, the number 1 is above the 118. If you look over at the left hand side, that has the names of the day signs, you will see that I am a Flint.

This is the method that you use to find your day sign and number.

Sacred Tzolkin

Sacred Sun Sign	(Spiritual Occupation)												Kin or Day Number
Crocodile	(1) 1	(8) 21	(2) 41	(9) 61	(3) 81	(10) 101	(4) 121	(11) 141	(5) 161	(12) 181	(6) 201	(13) 221	(7) 241
Wind	(2) 2	(9) 22	(3) 42	(10) 62	(4) 82	(11) 102	(5) 122	(12) 142	(6) 162	(13) 182	(7) 202	(1) 222	(8) 242
Night	(3) 3	(10) 23	(4) 43	(11) 63	(5) 83	(12) 103	(6) 123	(13) 143	(7) 163	(1) 183	(8) 203	(2) 223	(9) 243
Seed	(4) 4	(11) 24	(5) 44	(12) 64	(6) 84	(13) 104	(7) 124	(1) 144	(8) 164	(2) 184	(9) 204	(3) 224	(10) 244
Serpent	(5) 5	(12) 25	(6) 45	(13) 65	(7) 85	(1) 105	(8) 125	(2) 145	(9) 165	(3) 185	(10) 205	(4) 225	(11) 245
Transformer	(6) 6	(13) 26	(7) 46	(1) 66	(8) 86	(2) 106	(9) 126	(3) 146	(10) 166	(4) 186	(11) 206	(5) 226	(12) 246
Deer	(7) 7	(1) 27	(8) 47	(2) 67	(9) 87	(3) 107	(10) 127	(4) 147	(11) 167	(5) 187	(12) 207	(6) 227	(13) 247
Star	(8) 8	(2) 28	(9) 48	(3) 68	(10) 88	(4) 108	(11) 128	(5) 148	(12) 168	(6) 188	(13) 208	(7) 228	(1) 248
Offering	(9) 9	(3) 29	(10) 49	(4) 69	(11) 89	(5) 109	(12) 129	(6) 149	(13) 169	(7) 189	(1) 209	(8) 229	(2) 249
Dog	(10) 10	(4) 30	(11) 50	(5) 70	(12) 90	(6) 110	(13) 130	(7) 150	(1) 170	(8) 190	(2) 210	(9) 230	(3) 250
Monkey	(11) 11	(5) 31	(12) 51	(6) 71	(13) 91	(7) 111	(1) 131	(8) 151	(2) 171	(9) 191	(3) 211	(10) 231	(4) 251
Road	(12) 12	(6) 32	(13) 52	(7) 72	(1) 92	(8) 112	(2) 132	(9) 152	(3) 172	(10) 192	(4) 212	(11) 232	(5) 252
Reed	(13) 13	(7) 33	(1) 53	(8) 73	(2) 93	(9) 113	(3) 133	(10) 153	(4) 173	(11) 193	(5) 213	(12) 233	(6) 253
Jaguar	(1) 14	(8) 34	(2) 54	(9) 74	(3) 94	(10) 114	(4) 134	(11) 154	(5) 174	(12) 194	(6) 214	(13) 234	(7) 254
Eagle	(2) 15	(9) 35	(3) 55	(10) 75	(4) 95	(11) 115	(5) 135	(12) 155	(6) 175	(13) 195	(7) 215	(1) 135	(8) 255
Wisdom	(3) 16	(10) 36	(4) 56	(11) 76	(5) 96	(12) 116	(6) 136	(13) 156	(7) 176	(1) 196	(8) 216	(2) 136	(9) 256
Earth	(4) 17	(11) 37	(5) 57	(12) 77	(6) 97	(13) 117	(7) 137	(1) 157	(8) 177	(2) 197	(9) 217	(3) 237	(10) 257
Flint	(5) 18	(12) 38	(6) 58	(13) 78	(7) 98	(1) 118	(8) 138	(2) 158	(9) 178	(3) 198	(10) 218	(4) 238	(11) 258
Storm	(6) 19	(13) 39	(7) 59	(1) 79	(8) 99	(2) 119	(9) 139	(3) 159	(10) 179	(4) 199	(11) 219	(5) 239	(12) 259
Sun	(7) 20	(1) 40	(8) 60	(2) 80	(9) 100	(3) 120	(10) 140	(4) 160	(11) 180	(5) 200	(12) 220	(6) 240	(13) 260

DAY SIGNS

In what Ian used to call Gregorian astrology, the astrological system of the western world, the astrology signs are named after Greek and Roman gods and goddesses. This was the way that these ancient cultures were able to personify the energies that come from the planets in the solar system. The astrological sign of Aries is named after the Roman god of war and represents Mars, the planet of warrior energy. Venus is named after the Roman goddess of Love. The energy of the planets in our solar system do have an influence upon us. Astrology has long been a way to describe the influence that these heavenly bodies have on humanity.

The Maya created their own system based on the effects that the energy from the Hu Nab Ku or center of the Milky Way has upon us. The Maya, as did the earlier cultures of Mesoamerica, identified these influential energies and gave them names and identities to correspond with their environment and cosmology. The Maya describe these energies, when they manifest on our planet,as a Nawal. A Nawal or day sign is the form that the galactic energies take here on the Earth. Most have names of animals such as Jaguar or Eagle. Some like Wind, describe a force of nature or like Night, a time of day. The order of the day signs is very important as well. As you read through the different day signs, you will see that they go from a very primitive state of evolution, starting with Crocodile, to the final day sign, Sun, which represents the lineage of human beings.

The following day signs have the English name and then the Kiche Maya and Yucatec Maya name followed by the color and direction associated with each sign.

Crocodile, Imox, Imix Direction=Red/East

In many of the ancient codices that were found by the Spanish, Crocodile is the first or primal day sign. The day sign of Crocodile represents the Divine Mother. The dark rift in the center of the Milky Way represents the womb of the Divine Mother. The long, graceful body of the Crocodile resembles the dark rift in the Milky Way. Even if a man is born under the day sign of Crocodile, he will have strong connections to his family and will be very nurturing.

Crocodile people are very good at starting projects. The Crocodile is hard working and needs to be active. Their connection to the direction of the East, usually manifests in Crocodile and other fire signs as the desire to be active and create.

The East is also where the sun rises and therefore represents beginning. This is why Crocodiles need to be close to their support group or family structure. They need the help of the family energy to finish projects and be successful. Crocodiles are often motivated by those close to them. When the will of the Crocodile is focused for helping their loved ones, they can create great abundance and prosperity. Crocodiles make great farmers and builders. They are great at having their own businesses.

Even though the family or family - like unit, is very important to them, they do need to have their quiet time.

The crocodile person is a very hard worker. Yet, when they have exhausted themselves, the Crocodile may need to sink into the depths of the quiet waters to find balance and rejuvenation. A common pattern for the Crocodile is to work to their limit and then sink into a rest period. This may cause many people to think that the Crocodile is lazy. They are really just in touch with their body and know that they need to revive themselves.

In the time of the height of the Mayan empire, Crocodiles were great warriors. Crocodiles are known for their courage and valor. They will fight for their country, which is an extension of the family. When there is a crisis, the Crocodile person may be the first one to plunge in and help bring life back into balance. Crocodiles also feel a very strong connection to the earth. They receive energy and renewal from spending time out in nature. Famous Crocodiles are Walt Disney, Johnny cash and Aretha Franklin.

It is best that the Crocodile person follow their heart instead of their logic. When a Crocodile listens to their feelings they avoid confused thinking. The Crocodile person is also very in tune with their dreams and imagination. They are attracted to mystery, novels, illusion and other forms of escapism.

Crocodile people can be very dominating and angry. They can be difficult to work with. The domination factor also rears its ugly head when it comes to romantic relationships. It is important to realize that Crocodiles are doing this because they want to create a wonderful lair for those that are important to them. When the Crocodile energy is harnessed they can achieve great things. Other emotional traits of the Crocodile are that they have a hard time dealing with criticism. Yet they can be very critical and fussy when it comes to others.

The part of the body that is governed by Crocodile is the liver.

Wind, IQ, IK
Direction=White/North

It is not hard to imagine the nature of this day sign. It represents the movement and flow of the currents of the wind. The day sign Wind represents all forms of communication and travel. The direction of the North represents the mind or thought.

Wind people are spontaneous, freedom loving and changeable. They may spend their whole life without ever setting down roots. They are also known for being inconsistent. Their moods change from day to day or even hour to hour. Those that are close to Wind people may feel that they are living or working with a different person every day. They may be cool and detached one day and very impassioned, artistic and spiritual the next.

These people are very volatile when it comes to losing their temper. They may be laughing one minute and raging with anger the next. Wind people can also suffer from overindulgence of addictive behaviors. To others they may seem focused and alert, but within them is a hurricane of thoughts swirling around them that can often cause them to feel unclear on a path of action.

The energy of the Wind day sign also gives these people great physical agility. They may be good dancers, massage therapists or be interested in Yoga. Even with all these ups and downs, Wind people make excellent communicators. Teaching, journalism, and TV reporting are some of the fields where a Wind person will excel. Wind people are the original multi-taskers. Famous Wind people are Michael Jackson and Liz Taylor.

One thing is for sure, Wind people are very intelligent and have a lot of mental interests. During the course of their lives they may have more than one profession. They are the most resilient of all the day signs. They can make their way through a variety of situations and come out well. They can be very good with math. The changeable nature of investing in the stock market appeals to them. Those around them may think of them as unsure and inconsistent, but the Wind person always feels confident and self-assured. This is because they understand the selective process that is going on within them, even if the outside world does not.

The Wind born is often afraid of commitment and responsibility. Some flee from confrontation, some seek it out. They have been called fickle before. If you can live with the inconsistencies and changeability of Wind people, you will be entertained with a spontaneous, multi talented and exciting person that will never bore you. They may not know a lot about a few things, but they usually know a little about a lot of different subjects. The part of the body that governs the Wind is the mouth.

Night, Aq'ab'al, Akbal
Direction=Blue/West

This day sign represents the time of transition between day and night, dawn and dusk. It is at this time, according to many spiritual traditions, that the earth is most powerful. It is a time for magic. Most Mayan ceremonies, including the ceremony to welcome each new Mayan week, take place at dawn. That is why the day sign of Night is capable of communication with spirits and the underworld. Day sign Night is governed or influenced by the direction of the West. The West is the realm of the sub conscious, or to the Maya, the underworld. Those born in this day sign often have the gift of healing and prophecy. A Night person is good at connecting with the subconscious. A prominent Night person, Joseph Campbell, is famous for his study of mythology. His career is based on discussing what comes from the inner recesses of the psyche. Another master of illusion was author Jack Kerouac.

Night is one of the day signs that have the body lightening, or energy that comes spontaneously out of them. The parts of the body connected with Night are the eyes. Those born under this day sign are usually very attractive, with striking or mesmerizing eyes. Because the day sign of Night flirts with the darkness and all that is in it, Night people can find themselves lost in illusion, fantasy and addictive behaviors. Gambling can be a big problem for Night people. If Night people put their attention to spiritual matters or a business that has a spiritual focus, they can garner success.

When Night people get in touch with reality, they can become very wealthy through focus and hard work. They don't seek out fame and power, but they can handle it when it comes to them. The Night born is capable of very deep thought. Logic, organization, patience and endurance are some of the beneficial qualities of the Night person. They can become teachers, leaders and sometimes healers. Night likes to be of service.

They are the opposite of the Wind persona in that they like to stay home, create security and structure their life in a practical and orderly way. If they are clear on their goals, Night people will stay focused on a goal until completion, even if it takes many years to do so. These people can do very well in real estate. Night people usually feel the desire to have security, and they have the stamina to carry it through. Night people like to be creative with their homes. Their connection to the sub conscious also gives them a creative flair. Night people are also very private. They are romantic and are usually lucky in love even with their desire for privacy and alone time. Good luck follows them throughout their life.

These people can live happy, prosperous lives if they are willing to harness the power within them.

Seed, K'at, Kan
Direction=Yellow/South

This day sign has also been called by the name of net and lizard. I feel that Seed is the most appropriate name for this day sign because it represents the seed that grows into a corn stock. Therefore, Seed represents fertility. The main motivating energy of Seed is to start or bring together what is necessary to initiate new ideas. It is governed by the direction of the South, which represents the body and innocence. Seed people are usually very sexual people. They tend to have strong sexual and creative outlets for their passions. They need to redirect their primal energy to focus on their goals outside the bedroom.

The Seed nature is very connected to rhythm and therefore is a natural with music, dance and other rhythmic activities. They are also very individualistic and unconventional. They often end up, without any premeditation, to be very original or creative people with dynamic and attention-grabbing personas. Seed people don't care much about what others think of them, they are motivated by the driving force of the earth itself to bring who they feel they are inside to their outside. They love to express themselves through dress and costume. They may also feel that they are above the law, and like to make their own rules for life.

This Seed quality was very evident in the life of rock star Jim Morrison. It was a shame that he was not able to channel the tremendous force of the Seed nature into areas that promoted his personal happiness and wellbeing. He was not able to redirect his passions in a way that kept his excesses from being self destructive. Like Jim Morrison, Seed people have little control in many areas of life. Their tendency toward over indulgence may lead them to very extravagant life styles. It is a day sign that can attract a great deal of debt. This can come from the feeling of Seed people that there is only now. They do not like to save for a rainy day, but want to be in the present and use all that is at their disposal.

Even with Seed's dynamic connection to what is primal, they have great minds when they are able to focus them toward abstract thought. Their innate understanding of the life force of creation can be directed toward spirituality and philosophy. Seed people also make excellent healers, midwives and herbalists. They can easily become an expert in their field when they stick to their goals. They are not flexible once they have made up their minds about a situation or course of action.

Again, using Jim Morrison as an example, Seed people need to be free to express themselves. Freedom is very important to Seed people. They want nothing to come between them and the creations they wish to manifest. They understand the concept of parenting that promotes the idea that a child needs to be free to find out who they are and what talents they possess.

The main challenge for a Seed person is to find the balance between self expression and self preservation.

When a Seed person can bring their lives into a balance of physical, mental and emotional harmony, they can bring their dynamic perceptions to the planet and live to enjoy the satisfaction of their accomplishments. The part of the body that is represented by the Seed day sign are the hips.

The Seed persona is dynamic and oriented toward performance. Most Seed people want to lead healthy, balanced lives where they can express their individuality and sensuality. Their inner drive can be harnessed to bring them comfort and stability.

They do have difficulty with compromise, however. Always try to help the Seed person feel that their compromise is their idea, and then they will not feel frustrated. In terms of relationship, Seed people are happiest when they are able to feel free to express themselves sexually. They usually need to be in an unconventional relationship that allows them to be themselves.

Another powerful attribute of Seed people, namely leadership and fighting to liberate others, can be seen through the life of another famous Seed person: Martin Luther King. Seed people have high standards that they want to achieve for others as well as themselves. Mr. King represented the highest potential of a person born into the Seed day sign. He wanted to raise the quality of life for his people. Even after his death, his ideals have been carried on to fight for freedom of the oppressive patterns that had been created in the past. Seed people are also natural net workers.

Serpent, Kan, Chicchan - Direction=Red/East

Serpent is another very sensual, strong and healthy day sign. Like the rhythmic, even hypnotic movements of the snake, you will find many Serpent people in professions where flowing movement is basic to their work. I know a very interesting belly dancer who fits perfectly into her day sign of Serpent. She is charismatic and sexual, whether she is dancing or not.

The famous Serpent, Marilyn Monroe, is an example of a Serpent person that had tremendous sexual appeal that became larger than life. A career in entertainment, dance, music, teaching or politics comes easy to them. The part of the body that governs the energy of the Serpent is the genitals. Serpents can often get into complications due to their sex appeal. Many Serpents do not realize the power that they have and often become the victims of their sexual passions.

The Serpent projects their inner thoughts outside of themselves, even when they are not trying to do so. Those around them can feel their inner attitudes. Serpents do have very strong emotions that can bring upheaval to relationships and careers. When a Serpent has been drinking or under great pressure, these feelings will come to the surface. To nurture themselves through unpleasant emotional experiences, the Serpent person may use food, sex, artistic expression, computer games or even work to sooth themselves. Addictions may be something that Serpents need to acknowledge and maintain in balance.

They are fascinated with sex and with death and can devote much of their lives to these areas of experience. This manifests with Serpents as a very strong spiritual side that focuses on the essence of regeneration. They are connected with the concept of death and rebirth, primarily because they shed their skin and are in a sense, reborn. They have the ability to become psychics, communicate with the dead, shed light on past lives and interpret dreams. They may transmute into many careers and lifestyles throughout their lives.

The primal power of the Serpent can become very painful for those around them. Serpent people are influenced by the direction of the East that represents fire. Therefore, they can have fiery tempers. The Serpent is also very strong willed. If these people are not in integrity and do not have a spiritual focus, they can lead others into many agonizing problems.

Serpents must nurture themselves in order to stay in harmony with the world. Many Serpents go into a career that focuses on some aspect of Psychology. The shedding of the old to allow the new to emerge, like the snake shedding its skin, is an aspect of life that the Serpent person understands on a deep level. That is why they can be helpful to those who want to go through the transmutation process. Serpents also have a great desire to obtain many different types of knowledge. Their thirst for knowledge can make them natural educators. Some Serpents can become obsessive in their pursuit of wisdom.

They have great stamina that gives them the ability to keep doing strenuous activities for long periods of time. Serpents do need take time out to rest and regenerate in order to stay balanced .Most Serpents are healthy and this can give them great longevity. Serious illnesses may develop for a Serpent person who remains out of balance.

This captivating nature of the Serpent makes it possible for them to make great leaders. Leadership comes naturally to Serpents. They have great intellectual ability as well as instinctual strength. If a Serpent person gets to a position of power, it is important for them to be able to look beyond their own feelings and instincts to the needs of others. The charismatic nature of Serpent imbues them with a larger than life persona that translates to the stage, film and other industries where a strong presence is valuable. Mae West and Grace Kelly are two such Serpents that had a facade that made them famous. The magical, hypnotic quality of the Serpent can lead others to greatness or ruin. Most Serpent people do have an inner sense of law and justice that usually helps to keep them on track even in the face of temptation.

Transformer, Keme, Cimi
Direction=White/North

When Ian got back from working with the Mayan shaman, he knew that this day sign was called Death. He felt, and I did also at the time, that it might be scary for people to think that they were represented by Death. That is why we changed the name to Transformer. This word carries the idea that Transformer is really just a transition or transformation of the soul from the physical body to the realms of spirit.

For the Maya, the day sign of Transformer is a very productive, happy and prosperous one. Transformer people are known to be materialistic, security minded, helpful and accepting of change. They do not like to take a lot of risks. Transformer is associated with wealth and good luck. This is because the day sign Transformer is one of the few day signs, along with Night, Dog and Jaguar that can travel to the underworld, where all the riches of the earth are stored. Down below the surface of the earth lays the precious minerals that nourish the soil and cause the crops to grow. The underworld is where all the gold, silver and precious gems are stored. The day sign Transformer can bring back these riches or manifest them in the upper world on which we live. That is why Transformer people are good with acquiring material abundance.

Those born to the day sign of Transformer can also go to the underworld to ask the gods there for healing. That is why those who are born on Transformer days are often healers, shamans and psychics. Due to the fact that Transformer people have a direct pipeline to the underworld or sub conscious, they are able to be emissaries to the Underworld. Transformer shamans often journey to the Underworld in behalf of others. In shamanic practices, this is done to bring back pieces of the soul that have been separated from a person through trauma or abuse. This technique is called Soul Retrieval. Illnesses are often cured by a shaman who heals a person's illness while journeying to the underworld.

Even if a Transformer person is not interested in spiritual or shamanic matters, they still feel comfortable in the quiet of the dark and behind the scenes. Transformer people do not like to be leaders. They will usually partner with a person that is strong and responsible, even if they aren't that way. Even though they are clever and sociable, they like to be the power behind the throne. They find it hard to speak their true feelings and will find another to speak for them. They often like to work for their community, but in a way were they will not stand out. Sometimes Transformer people can be very secretive and serious. This can often be difficult for many relationships. Even though Transformer people can be strong under adversity, if a Transformer person is pushed too far or taken advantage of, they can become violent.

Those born under the day sign of Transformer have a special connection with the earth. They may own a lot of real estate. You could say that they have the Midas touch. Usually everything they do in the business world turns to abundance. They also like to help their communitiy acquire wealth. They care about the needy and oppressed and will be devoted to assisting them in some way. Their perfectionist nature helps them to acquire wealth by helping them attend to details and make sure that projects are completed correctly. They are advocates of responsibility because they see that as an important quality that is necessary for the good of the community.

Some famous Transformer people are Paul McCarthy and Jane Fonda. They both have acquired great wealth, but you don't find them in the headlines too often, just when they are getting married or divorced.

This brings me to another topic: marriage. The Maya feel that a Transformer day in the Tzolkin is a good time to get married or sign a contract. A marriage performed on a Transformer day will ensure a happy and prosperous union. In many Mayan villages, a person born under the day sign of Transformer will be the village marriage broker. They like bringing fruitfulness to their community and to help people maintain the traditions of their culture.

Transformer people will work very hard for the good of their community. They feel that the community is an extension of them and therefore will put the effort and skill they have perfected for their own prosperity in effect for who or whatever they feel is their community. They are good writers and communicators so they often have an interest in politics; even if they do not take wish to be a political leader. A sense of duty and obligation to others are a very strong part of the Transformer personality. Even if they are experiencing adversity, Transformer people seem to have some divine protection and usually seem to come through life's storms without being washed away.

Deer, Kyej, Manik
Direction=Blue/West

The Mayan glyph for this day sign is a hand. Even though the English name is deer, I feel that it is important to realize that this day sign's great strength is that it cares for the well-being of others. The hand is a symbol of protection and support. "You are in good hands with Allstate". This is the basic foundation of the day sign Deer. The hand in the symbol is cupped or closed, implying that those born under this day sign are here to create a circle of protection and safety. They are peaceful, generous and cooperative.

Even though Deer people are often quiet, sensitive and creative, they usually are concerned with the wellbeing of others. They are a bit shy and do not like being a leader, but the welfare of a family or group of people that they care about is of utmost importance to them. In the time of the ancient Maya, those born under this day sign were hunters and rulers. They often sacrificed themselves for the sake of the community. Even though food is very important to Deer people, they made sure others were fed before they were. This strength and authority can often seem like domination to many who are around them.

With this in mind, it is easy to see that the nature of the hunter and wanderer are part of the Deer psyche. Even though the Deer is very community oriented, they have a great need to travel. Deer often becomes a world traveler. They may have spent a good portion of their younger days living in foreign countries. They thrive on the stimulation from foreign cultures or even counter cultures.

The Deer person does have an artistic nature. They have a strong aesthetic side that can often lead them to be involved with and be a supporter of the arts. They may devote themselves to the arts, music, poetry and writing. They also have a strong sense of intuition. Yet dependency on the trappings of the psychic world, such as crystals and Tarot cards can take them away from and hinder the development of their true psychic abilities.

Those born under the day sign of Deer are also very sexual. Their need for freedom often makes is difficult for them to make lasting personal commitments, even though they are very committed to their community. One of the greatest challenges for a Deer person is to blend the need for community and the need for freedom into their lives. They are a contradiction of sorts, in that they want relationships, but value their freedom above all else.

The Deer born also need to learn how to be more flexible. They can get much attached to certain ideas or ways of being and find it difficult to be adaptable. Deer also suffers from procrastination. If they will create a plan or timetable for projects that need to be finished, they will be successful in completing what they want to achieve.

Pope John Paul was an example of a Deer person that worked for the greater good.

As you might imagine, the part of the body ruled by the day sign of Deer are the feet. Those feet like to travel. These people have the instinct to roam as all good hunters do. It is important for them to spend some time in Nature to keep in balance.

As you can tell from these descriptions, the Deer day sign is comprised of many contradictions. A Deer can be eccentric or peculiar. They can have strong beliefs that they will not give up, even if they are proved wrong. Deer people are, like many aspects of human life, confusing but wonderful.

Star, Quanil, Lamat
Direction=Yellow/South

This day sign represents the planet Venus and is therefore called Star. To the Maya, the planet Venus was associated with the myth of Kukulkan or Quetzalcoatl. The Morning Star phase of Venus represents an immature Kukulkan who participated in many types of debauchery including incest. Realizing his mistakes, Kukulkan sailed away in a boat set afire to die. The gods took pity on him and he was reborn, a healed man.

Many of the less productive traits of Kukulkan, such as drinking, gambling, drug abuse and other addictions can be part of the Star psyche. Many Star people like to be center stage and make a lot of money in this way. Their desire for attention can lead them into the entertainment fields. They love to experience or make music. Two examples of Star people are Elvis Presley and Jimmy Hendrix.

On the positive side, Star people are very energetic, playful and can be very good in business. They have a lot of nervous energy that they need to discharge in hopefully productive ways. They can do a lot of physical work without tiring. Those born under this day sign are very talented at making money. Star is one of the day signs that are related to the fruitfulness of the earth. They also like to bargain. They have been known to haggle over a price until they get the deal that they are seeking.

To a Star person, competition or pressing to win a game or debate is very important. They thrive on challenges, puzzles, and what it takes to solve them. They truly enjoy games, learning foreign languages, codes and other forms of problem solving. Star people can be very detail oriented. They like to be knowledgeable and exact. They can often be found in the investigation or intelligence fields of work. Star people also like to work with different forms of communication like writing and reading. Star people have a great appreciation for music. When they are not locked in a deliberation or contest, they have a great sense of humor.

Star people also have an interest in psychology and addiction healing. They will often be found in 12 step programs when they have conquered their inner demons and want to help others do the same.

Star people like to share their winnings and are usually very generous. They like luxury and like to share their harvest. If they are not kept busy, this desire for luxury can lead to overindulgence. The parts of the body that is ruled by the Star day sign are the ears.

Offering, Toj, Muluc
Direction=Red/East

The day sign of Offering has also been called Incense by some sects of the Maya. It is the incense that is burned by the fire of the East to bring about an offering. This day sign relates to the ceremonial aspect of life. It is only natural that Offering people are inclined to be performers or in some way up in front of the public. Offering people often carry the shame and trauma of the community or family. They are very charismatic, sexual and have very fiery emotions. Their extreme sensitivity can be a cause of their emotional flair ups. They take everything that happens to or around them very seriously. They possess a very powerful and sometimes hypnotic sex drive. This works well for them when they are up in front of the public. Two very noticeable people born under the day sign of Offering are Bill Clinton and Madonna.

Those born under this day sign are extremists in many ways. They often exhibit an all or nothing perspective for projects they take on. It is their passion for life that can propel them in to prominence, success or scandal. They are willing to take chances to manifest their creative vision and beliefs. They do enjoy the thrill of taking risks. Their strong emotional energy can lead to compulsive behavior and addictions to sex, drinking, money and drugs if it not channeled positively. They can also create a lot of debt for themselves if their passions are not kept in check. Some people will find the Offering person uncouth and a bit lacking in social decorum.

Offering people also possess a very strong and independent mind. They put this to work by combining their mental faculties with intuition to solve many problems with original ideas. They do not seek leadership, but once drawn into that arena of life, they may be powerful and successful.

Offering people usually have a powerful relationship with their mother. Some Offering people can be dominated by their mothers or hang on to them long after the apron strings should have been cut.

If Offering people can control their urges, they can get in touch with a very powerful spiritual nature within themselves. Many are very psychic and are interested in the fields of UFO and paranormal activity such as ghosts. While many feel that these areas of exploration are eccentric, Offering people are fascinated. They can lose themselves in fantasy due to their powerful imaginations.

Those that are involved with Offering people may find it necessary to reign them in from time to time. They do have a bit of an all or nothing mentality. When they get involved in something, they go whole hog. Helping an offering person see the bigger picture is for their own good.

When an Offering person is able to keep their emotions under control, as well as their spending, and narrow their focus, they can achieve great things. Offering people like to take risks with their time and money, so they need someone to help them have perspective in these areas. The part of the body that is ruled by Offering is the hair.

Dog, T'zi, Oc
Direction=White/North

The representation of the canine world comes to us through the day sign of Dog. To the Maya, those born under this day sign are kind, warm, loyal, friendly, cooperative and affectionate. This day sign is also very sexual. Ian use to say that Dog is the most sexual of all the day signs.

Dog people have a need to patrol the area that they call their home or territory. This causes Dog people to meander. This is why the Dog day sign is associated with travel. They also have a need to make sure that their territory is functioning up to their standards. They have to make sure that everyone within their domain is doing what they need to do and that the whole of the Dog world is functioning smoothly. This can translate into a Dog person being very concerned with all the people in their lives. Many times they may spend a lot of time with a friend or relative who is in need and may not have much time for their spouse or immediate family. They want to make everything right for others, but they have to allow people to regulate their lives by themselves.

Dog people like to be part of a family or group. In their own way, Dog people are very loyal. They do however, sometimes have a double standard: one for them and one for their mate and others in their family.

Dogs are pleasure seekers. The Dog person can be very jealous. They need clear boundaries in order to feel comfortable. Dog people usually have large families or social groups.

The good of the group is always a big concern to Dog people. They will work tirelessly to achieve prosperity or whatever is needed by the group or family. They will seek leadership roles if they arise. Even though they probably won't seek out leadership, they will wait until they are needed by the group. Dog people can be good leaders, but they do not usually create the cause for which they are fighting. They will stick to a cause and see it through to the end. This is another aspect of the loyalty of the Dog day sign.

Dog is considered, by the Maya, to be a prosperous day sign. The mythology behind this trait of Dog is that the ancient Maya considered the Dog to be a guide to the underworld, where all the riches of the planet can be found. A Dog person has the ability to find prosperity in whatever they do. They make very good employers, and can often be found in careers as judges, administrators and protectors. They find great fulfillment in the arts, especially music. They like short distance travel and many Dogs will have a love of cars. You may even be able to find a boat or plane in some Dog garages.

As you can imagine, the part of the body that is represented by Dog is the nose. Willy Nelson is a famous Dog who has done a great deal to further the cause of his group, those who create Country music.

Dogs also have a strong connection to the father energy. Dog people may have issues with their father growing up. If this connection is positive for the Dog person, they will be very successful in life. If there is trauma with their father figure, Dog people should seek to heal this relationship, whether their father is alive or dead. When this bond is healed, the Dog person will rise to the top of the pack and be of great value to their community as well as to themselves. Their connection to their father figure helps them achieve many of their goals.

Monkey, Batz, Chuen
Direction=Blue/West

The day sign of Monkey is very active, quick witted and lively. Monkey people like to bounce from one situation to another, like a monkey that likes to swing from tree to tree. You could say that they are mercurial in nature. They get bored doing the same thing all the time, so they need a great deal of variety in life to be in balance. They learn new things easily and will become frustrated with people in their lives that do not adapt to their constant flow of new ideas and activities. Monkeys are perfectionists and because they take to new situations and skills easily, they have to work at realizing that others do not take to new skills and situations as easily and quickly.

Even though the Monkey is lucky in the areas of love and money, they are a paradox when it comes to relationship. They have their social face or persona that they show to most people, but they have a very private side where they let it all hang out only to those they trust to honor what they may consider their down side. They like the attention that a committed relationship can offer. Yet, they have a hard time giving back the focus and connection that is necessary in a long term bond. Many Monkeys become distant and hard to pin down for holidays, events and other structured situations that are part of relationship. They can become bored or restless in long relationships. It is good to keep this in mind when you are considering tying the knot with a Monkey. It is important to accept the inconsistency of the Monkey nature if you are going to be involved with one. They are usually more active at night and like the night life. Some Monkeys never commit, because they like playing the field. They have a strong desire for sex and the attention it gives them. One thing is sure: you will always be entertained when a Monkey person is in your life.

They like to be independent and are always seeking a new group to perform in front of. Monkeys are naturally drawn to positions of leadership and politics. Sometimes, the Monkeys that get into leadership positions do not have the consistency to follow through and do justice to the positions that they have achieved. Even so, they get into politics and other areas where a dramatic personality is valuable. They become more involved in community and civic affairs as they get older.

Monkey people also make good actors, artists, musicians, writers and designers. Chuen people are good communicators. They make good teachers, lecturers and salespersons. Being up in front of an audience is the ultimate achievement for a Chuen person. That is why they make great performers. It is in the basic Monkey nature to imitate or reproduce what they see in the world. Many areas of art, where the hands are used, are very appealing careers to the Monkeys. They can be very good with details.

Monkeys have a great sense of humor. Sometimes this can manifest as a Monkey who likes to play a lot of practical jokes. Any area of life, where the Monkey can capture the attention of their audience, is where a Monkey person will naturally go.

These people can often be hyperactive and may have trouble staying with a project. They are very good at starting things. It will not be a surprise to people that are strongly connected to a Monkey person that they will have to help them or even take over a project that a Monkey person has started. The Monkey day sign is ruled by the West, the place of hibernation and rest. That is why it is good for a Monkey person to rest and regroup when they are feeling over stimulated or out of control. If they retreat to the quiet and darkness of the West, they will be able to regenerate and come back to their charismatic and dynamic self. It is their connection to the sub conscious that is represented by the West, which gives them their creative nature.

It is important for the Monkey person not to lose perspective and take themselves too seriously. This was the case with famous Monkey Charles Manson. Barbara Streisand and Ronald Reagan are other Monkey people who have been very successful in their lives. The parts of the body that are associated with Monkey are the hands.

Road, E, Eb
Direction=Yellow/South

Road people are the opposite of the agitated monkey. They are humble, relaxed and courteous. They like to be generous and expect little or nothing in return. Ian used to say that Road people are like the simple plant grass. They cover the earth, are not complicated and find it easy to survive and flourish everywhere. Road people are in tune with the energy of renewal. When there has been a fire in an area, grass is the first plant to grow again.

Being that they are ruled by the direction of the South, Road people like to do practical work that keeps them in touch with their body and the earth. Road people will work hard for the sake of others. They will work tirelessly for the ones they love. They will dedicate themselves to creating prosperity and comfort for loved ones. They will put steady effort into their goals until they manifest. They will even make great sacrifices to achieve prosperity for those who are in their personal lives.

Their romantic and family life is very important to them. When a Road person makes sacrifices for others they often get their feelings hurt. They need to feel that their work for others is appreciated. If they do not get this appreciation, they can harbor feelings of resentment and anger. This is because they are very sensitive and even small things may hurt their feelings. They can also be very opinionated and find it difficult when those that they make sacrifices for do not embrace their ideals. They are usually very easy going and it takes a lot for a Road person to express their negative feelings. If they feel appreciated and encouraged, Road people can climb to great heights.

Two examples of Road people are Hugh Heffner and Ross Periot. As you can see with Hugh Heffner, he is very successful but likes to live in an atmosphere that is quiet and hidden away from the world. Road people can create the stage, but they usually do not like to be on it. Like most Road people, Hugh Heffner is also very sexual but doesn't like to be in the spotlight all the time.

Those born under the Road day sign have a very strong spiritual side. Even though they are very practical and down to earth, they have a strong psychic sense. That is why they are very successful in careers that deal with advertising and promotion. We can see that Hugh Heffner turned a girlie magazine into a worldwide promotional machine.

Even with Mr. Heffner's interest in having sex with many women, he still has tried to have relationships over the years. Road people like one on one romance but like Hugh, they also like to have large parties with many people relating in a pleasant manner. Road people are very peaceful, kind and find that many people like to be around them, even though they do not like to seek out attention.

Road people have a close connection with fertility. They have a strong connection to the environment. They make good mid wives for they are attuned to the birth and growth process. They also make excellent parents. They usually make sure that their children have good manners, which is very important to the Road psyche. In the Mayan communities, Road people are often the tribe's healer. They are able to bring out the body lightening for healing and benefit of others.

Road people may be faced with many health challenges throughout their life. This often motivates them to seek out natural forms of healing. The Road born is very good at administering herbal remedies. Road people also have an interest in ancient spiritual knowledge. They like finding ancient teachings or knowledge and putting this information to good use.

As you can imagine, Road people like to travel with those they love. They are by nature curious and enjoy exploring. This gives them a natural ability in the areas where attention to details, solving problems and engineering are important.

The part of the body that is associated with Road is the stomach.

Reed, Aj, Ben
Direction=Red/East

The job of many Reed people is to be an intermediary in many situations. They can be helpful with arguments and other types of conflicts of daily life. Reed people do not seek out conflict, but some aspect of themselves thrives on participating in a clash and seeing it resolved. They are ruled by the direction of the East and they are good at initiating change in stagnant situations. Ian would say that the Reed people can be in the water and in the air, so they are good at helping people see and accept differences in another's worlds. In many Mayan tribes, Reed people have the position of the tribe elder or wise man. The Reed persona rarely exhibits emotion under duress. That is why they make good mediators.

Reed people are usually way ahead of their time and often are able to be successful by giving humanity something that is new and unique. Reeds can be risk takers or ground breakers in many areas of life. The Reed personality is motivated by an underlying desire to achieve and manifest new products and services. They can bring innovation to whatever arena of life is their focus, be it career or family. This is why they can be thought of as an expert in whatever they chose to feel is their field of competency. Reeds are dignified and esteemed in their community. They can turn into perfectionists and if not checked, can have extremist viewpoints. The Reed personality loves to relax and enjoy life, but they can be extremely focused and capable of working hard in necessary. This tendency brings them high regard in their community and they tend to be well liked.

Some Reeds go on to have political careers because they are concerned with justice. They are insightful and dedicated. Reeds are deep thinkers. They often seek out careers as researchers and psychologists. This tendency can also translate to an interest in philosophy and religion. They like to communicate what they have learned or what they find interesting. This desire to communicate and to work for change can be seen in the politicians Jerry Brown, who was the governor of California and Sonny Bono, who became the mayor of Palm Springs, CA. Like Jerry Brown, the Reed person will stick with an issue until their goals are achieved. Again, like Mr. Brown, they can be crusaders and even politically unpopular when they are working for what they feel is the good of others.

Reed is another day sign that may need to have a lot of freedom in order to achieve what is important to them. They have such a broad range of interests. They need to have the freedom to pursue the many projects that fascinate them. Even though they feel hearth and home to be very important, and are not big travelers by nature, they have a lot of energy due to their fire element.

Reeds are usually prosperous because they are imbued with the fire energy of the East and like to be productive. When they feel they are on the right track, they can bring many innovations to the world. Their openness to new ideas can put them at the forefront of many fields.

They have a natural inner confidence that helps people feel confident about them. Reeds are usually good parents for they have the ability to see the qualities of each child and the ability to bring harmony to their family. Mia Farrow is Reed person who is very dedicated to the dynamics of a large family.

The downside of Reed people is that they can be rigid and opinionated. This quality can often make it difficult for them to honor their highest potential. They need a lot of appreciation and pats on the back when they have been successful in order to stay in balance. The part of the body that is connected with Reed is the spleen.

Jaguar, IX
Direction=White/North

In the way that a Reed person likes to be a public figure and out among the people, those born under the Jaguar day sign tend to be secretive and like to hide in the cover of the night. The Jaguar born is good at professions that thrive on secrecy such as security work or investigations. They are patient as they wait for the information that they are seeking for themselves or others. Jaguar people are in touch with the underworld. They are one of the day signs that can travel to the underworld and come back with the riches stored there. Jaguars are often very good at making money.

Jaguar is ruled by the North, the direction of knowledge. Many Jaguars are very intelligent and well educated. They can become very powerful educators, writers, therapists and spiritual counselors. When the Jaguar sets their mind on a goal, they find it easy to manifest it. This is because they have a good sense of strategy and are excellent planners. They have great imaginations and a very artistically creative side. This expression of creativity may also stimulate their extravagant, indulgent side.

Jaguars usually are the shamans and healers of their Mayan tribe. They have the knowledge of the plant medicine. Their flirtation with the night makes Jaguar a great emissary to the underworld. Jaguar is able to journey to the underworld to fight on behalf of a client for pieces of their soul which is called Soul Retrieval in shamanic cultures.

Jaguar people are very skilled at using herbs and aromatherapy. Those born under the day sign of Jaguar are often the Day Keepers or the people that keep track of the count of the Tzolkin. Most Jaguars find it easy to become a priest, minister or other spiritual icon. Worship, devotion to the divine, ritual and ceremony are very important to them. Many make ceremony and ritual part of their daily life. They often hold the space for others to experience ceremony and ritual even if they are not leading it. The Jaguar born is very at home with spiritual or shamanic practices and feels they have a calling to perpetuate this knowledge. To the ancient Maya, the Jaguar priests were thought of as special and sacred members of their community.

Jaguar people are brave, courageous, forceful, and proud. They also possess great endurance. The Jaguar is one of the animals that is able to see in the dark and hunts at night. This is why they can perceive what may not be apparent to others. Therefore, Jaguar people are often very psychic. Even if they do not profess to be psychics, Jaguar people are able to receive information for others through their impressions or through dreams.

The Jaguar born is not usually a leader or seeker of attention. Just the opposite, they need to be hidden or at least not noticeable. They like to support their community and will help others, but do not like to be the center of attention. They often become an anonymous benefactor that asks for nothing in return. A famous Jaguar was Richard Nixon. We all know that he had a lot of hidden secrets! The parts of the body that are associated with Jaguar are the feet.

Other qualities of the Jaguar include a quick temper and a bit of vanity. They also like competition. As you can tell from these descriptions, Jaguars have a magical side that is very inviting to children. If they have children, they understand their world and make good parents.

Eagle, Tz'kin, Men
Direction=Blue/West

The day sign Eagle is a very powerful one to the Maya, as well as many other indigenous traditions. The Eagle is an escapist. They like to soar above and way from much of humanity. That is why they have a connection to the West. They are often in tune with what many others cannot see or know. It is not uncommon for Eagle people to be thought of as advisors. Their quest for truth and knowledge is often a lifelong pursuit. The Eagle has a unique presence that can be dramatic and other worldly. Even though they are very friendly and well liked, they can be shy and very private about their personal life.

The paradox here is that Eagles are very social and are usually popular and have many friends. Eagle people are often leaders. Many see them as proud and courageous. They are also clever and honest. The bravado of their personality can bring adoration and even hero worship. John Fitzgerald Kennedy was an Eagle who saw great possibilities for the United States and the world. Like JFK, Eagles do like to bend the rules when they feel it is beneficial to them.

Eagles have a perspective that those tied to the ground do not have. It is not unusual for an Eagle person to have ideas or projects that are way ahead of their time. They are best when they are free to soar above the rest of the world. They can see potentials that most of us are not aware of. This is why Eagle people are often wealthy and successful. They are able to attune to future financial potentials and use them.

Even though Eagle people are able to see the big picture better them most, they are also very detailed oriented. The eagle is able to see its dinner walking around on the ground when it is far up in the sky. They have perfectionist tendencies. They can be very precise teachers, writers and communicators. They make excellent architects and engineers. They also make excellent inventors. They can develop products that society does not even know it needs yet.

Those born under the day sign of Eagle also have a strong warrior spirit. They will fight for a cause that they feel is right. They are not interested in competition, however. They like to avoid confrontation and competition, but when it is necessary to compete, they become very focused on winning or achieving their goals. It is not good for an Eagle person to become too fixated on any particular person, place or object. Tunnel vision is the bane of their lives. Eagles do best when they are their own bosses.

Eagle people do not do well in close relationships. Eagles usually have their own set of rules and standards that work for them which may be opposed to the ideals of their society. This can make for unusual, open relationships with those with whom they are close. They feel that they need to be free to be at their best and experience the great wonders of life. Eagles can be world travelers, for they love to be free to explore the world.

The part of the body that is ruled by the day sign Eagle is also the hands.

Wisdom, Ajmak, Cib
Direction=Yellow/South

The primary function of this day sign, which is ruled by the southern direction, is to be a cleanser and purifier of itself and of the world. This cleansing ability that Wisdom has is necessary as part of the cycle of rebirth. The themes of death and rebirth are very strong within the Wisdom psyche. Wisdom, or as some Maya call this sign, Vulture, frees the world of decay. This allows new growth to come into the world. Wisdom is concerned with material cleansing and therefore is concerned with cleansing the body physically and emotionally. Many times Wisdom people go into health fields to help others cleanse body and spirit.

Many Wisdom people, such as the famous Wisdom Robert Redford, fight to cleanse and purify the environment. He campaigns against all the pollutants and closed mindedness that have brought decay to our blessed Mother Earth. Their connection to this necessary aspect of life on the earth plane causes Wisdom people to be a bit on the serious side. Another aspect of the focus on purification that is part of the Wisdom persona is that they are able to release the Karma or debts of past actions. Wisdom people often take on the problems of others and help them to solve these problems. This happens because the Wisdom person is very psychic.

They feel the problems of others. Their basic nature is to be outspoken, so it is natural for them to want to help others by expressing their intuitive insights. Many times the Wisdom people become victims when they try to be of service.

Those born under Wisdom are, deep down, solemn. Even though many have a great sense of humor, their comic relief usually has a touch of sarcasm and cynicism. They are very pragmatic and usually have to work hard in life to achieve what may come easy to others. They are persistent and even though rising to the top may take a lot of work, Wisdom people are able to achieve a lot of their goals. Wisdom people can be very successful and status conscious. Their high standards and natural skills as managers and administrators enable them to rise to the top of any pecking order. When they get to the top, they may be a bit dominating. This is because they worked hard to get to the top and want to keep their structure in order. They also can be a bit vain and take a lot of pride in their accomplishments. They do have good taste and enjoy the finer things in life when they are able to obtain them. They make good advisors, and they naturally like to help people be successful.

Wisdom people often feel that they are carrying the burdens of the world on their backs. You will feel an underlying sadness about Wisdom people, even when they are having fun. These people have to be careful of not falling into the victim role or allow them to be used. Forgiveness is one of their greatest qualities, so even if they are used and abused, they do not hold a grudge for long.

Wisdom people are usually healthy and can enjoy their old age. They can be stern parents, but they will do anything for their family and friends. Wisdom needs to realize that they can be judgmental and critical, so they need to temper this when dealing with family and close friends. The part of the body that is associated with Wisdom is the ears. A Wisdom person is a great friend that will listen to all your problems and try to help you solve some of them.

Earth, N'oj, Caban
Direction=Red/East

This day sign has been connected with earthquake and movement in the ancient Aztec system, and to the Maya, the name means earth. The Maya considered this a good day sign for commerce, medicine and matchmaking. All of these practices take a clever mind, which is the primary trait of Earth people. They are deep thinkers that bubble over with many ideas. They represent the change and movement that the earth can create from within its fiery core. Sudden and unexpected change is a fundamental theme in the Earth life.

Those born under the day sign of Earth have as their strongest attribute their desire for knowledge. They have very quick minds and are therefore connected with the fire energy and the direction of the East. They can be passionate and even overwhelming when they want to communicate their ideas or beliefs. They are usually very talented, practical, clever and active. These qualities also correspond with the fire energy. They are freedom loving and need to be in motion. Their busy minds may shift focus often. They are able to see situations from many perspectives.

Their impassioned thoughts and ideas can lead to clashes with those who cannot accept their progressive perspectives. Timothy Leary is an example of an Earth person whose radical beliefs have shaken up and changed our world. Earth people are very wrapped up in their thoughts. They often go on tangents. They can also be brutally honest and lacking in tact. Many who observe them feel that they are on a mental rollercoaster. All of their mental activity can wear them out, and they can become very fragile. They can have a great sense of humor if they are going in a positive direction. Earth needs to take mental vacations from time to time, so as to keep in balance and not be overwhelmed by all their ideas.

Due to their love of thought, Earth people make good teachers as well as religious leaders. Timothy Leary was both. Sometimes Earth people will take their ideals to civil life and become politicians. They can be very inspiring communicators and can make effective political representatives. They prefer to be a leader rather than a follower. Their ideas can also be found in the area of the arts, especially music. They love to read and explore the ideas of others. Earth people also make great engineers and strategists. In order for Earth people to be most effective, they need to stay focused. When they do this, they can manifest their lofty ideals.

Earth people have high standards as parents and often do not understand their children's desires for conformity. The stubborn side of Earth people can create conflict with children who want to go their own way. Earth people are very loyal and will stay in a marriage or relationship to the end.

If Earth people are able to stand back and let others share their thoughts and views, there can be great understanding and appreciation. If you can convince an Earth person that your plans have merit, they will be your greatest supporter.

Flint, Tijax, Etznab
Direction=White/North

During the time of the ancient Maya, the flint or Obsidian blade that had many purposes. It was a finely carved instrument that was used to kill sacrificial victims and remove their beating hearts during ceremony. That is why this day sign has been associated with sacrifice. The flint or Obsidian blade was used by the commoner and the priest alike to perform various types of blood sacrifice rituals.

Those born under this day sign have the tendency to be keepers of spiritual traditions and healers. They make great teachers of all types of knowledge, spiritual or mundane. There are many psychics born to this day sign. This day sign is a great fighter for a cause that they believe in. A Flint person, though often quiet, polite and self-sacrificing, will fight for what they feel is important. They will fight to reveal injustice and discrimination in any area of life. They will take their fight as far as they can.

Their desire for knowledge that is correct and useful is why they are associated with the direction of the North that is the domain of the mind. They have a big interest in the mental arena of life. They are voracious readers and love to explore new subjects. They can become well versed and even experts in many arenas of life. They enjoy helping people solve problems. They do have a practical side. They like seeing a practical application to their ideas and interests. They are usually well coordinated, if not mechanically inclined.

Flint people are good communicators, counselors. They can also be thought of as physical and emotional healers. Their flair for communication will guide them into the realms of emotional and psychological careers. The flint or Obsidian blade was carried by the warrior but was also used by the surgeon to cut out infection or tumors. A Flint person can help you cut out physical and emotional chaos that is causing you pain.

Flint people do have their own personal tribulations. They may often suffer from struggle and hardship when they are young. This tends to give them a well-seasoned exterior that many will feel is blunt and aloof. It is good for Flint people to try to soften this exterior for it holds people at a distance.

The Flint person can have an explosive temper. They will often suppress their feelings or make sacrifices to keep the peace. Then, when they can swallow no more, they spew forth a lot of negative words that could have been better expressed when the situation first came up. Addressing issues as they arise is a great challenge yet the pathway to their happiness.

Gossip, or negative communication, is the blight upon the life of Flint person. They become involved in it and then they always seem to be blamed when the information gets to the person they are discussing. It is best for Flint people to remember that if they can't say anything nice, don't say anything at all. This will keep them in balance and give them the harmony that they so greatly desire.

Flint people are very at home with gatherings, alliances and love affairs. They can be the ideal friend and lover. They enjoy cooperation. They love to help others, but must do this without losing their center or sense of self. The part of the body that is connected with Flint is the mouth. That is why Flint people can be very powerful teachers, writers, singers and even politicians. This day sign also find satisfaction in engineering, photography and the arts.

Those born under the day sign of Flint are very concerned with their work and also with their appearance. Woman born under this day sign are often very attractive or compelling in some way. Vanity is often a word that is associated with Flint people. Sophia Loren and Cher are two well-known Flint women.

Storm, Kawuk, Cauac
Direction=Blue/West

This day sign represents the movement of the water in our world. Many times they attract turbulence, even though they do not create it. This is part of the Storm nature. It might be better to call this day sign Lighting Rod, because they always attract intensity to their lives. Two famous Storm people are Princess Diana and Yoko Ono.

Storm is associated with the direction of the West. This is because Storm people have a strong connection with the sub conscious. To the Maya, this is a connection to the Underworld. Storm people have a strong sense of intuition. They can be very psychic when necessary. Many Storm people are drawn to the study of religion, spirituality and philosophy. Other aspects of the sub conscious, namely creativity and artistic ability are also part of the Storm makeup. Some Storm people put this to use as an artist. They are most drawn to Psychology or some type of emotional healing modality. Storm people also make excellent teachers. They are good listeners and can make great counselors.

The day sign Storm feels that romantic relationship is very important in their lives. Relationship can act as an anchor to keep them on track. They fall in love quickly and deeply. Their perspective on sex is that it is a spiritual and honored experience. They are often interested in spiritually based sexual practices. They are very monogamous. They demand fidelity.

It is in the Storm nature to be loving, affectionate and compassionate. They are very supportive emotionally, be it to friends or family. They have great concern for the welfare of others and often do volunteer work.

Storm people are very good at details and can be good writers and teachers. They can see things from many different angles. They are curious and have a lot of interests. They are able to take someone else's ideas and improve on them. Storm people often activate or bring out the best in others. They can be easily influenced by others and need to be selective about who and what they bring into their lives.

Storm people can be plagued with addictions, if they are not functioning at their highest frequency. In other areas of health, Storm people can suffer from many ailments that can become chronic illnesses if they are not treated in their early stages. This need to transform health issues can lead Storm people to be interested in different types of healing and purification including fasting and stress release techniques. Some Storm people will turn this interest in healing into a career and become doctors and midwives. Their emotional energy can cause them to become very empathic. In whatever area of life the Storm person chooses to receive abundance, they are usually successful and prosperous.

There is a very happy and playful side of the Storm personality. These people can be very childlike and innocent in nature. Their friendly, youthful and helpful personality makes them enjoyable to be around. The parts of the body that are associated with Storm are the eyes.

Sun, Ajpu, Ahau
Direction=Yellow/South

This is the day sign that Ian was born into. He fulfilled many of the Sun potentials during his time on the earth. Ian was able to get the information he did because those born under the Sun day sign commune with the ancestors. Sun people have a direct pipeline to the departed as well as spirit guides and other spiritual beings.

Aside from being a medium and clairvoyant, Sun people are very creative. They are poets, dancers, singers, artists and skilled craftspeople, especially jewelers. They can also be a bit theatrical. In the time of the ancient Maya, the kings were usually born into the day sign of Sun. The king had to be a creative person as well as a hunter and blow gunner. The Sun person may have to face many challenges in order to be able to manifest their greatness. They can be blinded by their ego and be self centered, if they are not careful.

In their personal lives, Sun people do not have an easy time in relationships. Even though a Sun person can be very gracious, polite and mannerly, they have very unrealistic ideals for their mates. This idealism is often found in their goals for their life as well. This can often lead them to be disillusioned and hurt when their ideals of love or career do not fully manifest. Often times they cannot live up to their own ideals of love and commitment.

Sun people are very sensual, sexual and romantic. This causes them to go with whoever crosses their path and they soon leave their ideals of commitment behind. Paradoxically, Sun is fascinated with human love and emotions. They enjoy exploring the intricacies of relationship. Even if they have their traumas with relationship, they can make good counselors.

A Sun's high ideals can lead them to have unexplained fears of the future. They need to feel secure with what is happening in the present and have clear plans for the future. Once they are committed to a course of action, they usually do not change their mind. They may often feel justified in using others when they feel that it is necessary to achieve their idealistic and sometimes unattainable goals. Sun people will often devote their lives to some ideal. Sometimes, as in Ian's case, their dedication can impact the world. Even with all of his disappointments, Ian was true to his love of the Maya until his death. The creation of the charts in this book have brought Mayan astrology to a large audience.

Albert Einstein and Vincent Van Gogh are examples of famous Sun people. The part of the body that is associated with Sun is the heart.

THE NUMBERS

Along with each of the day signs is a number between one and thirteen. The day sign and the number combine to create the primary astrology sign in Mayan astrology. The number or tones as they have come to be called, add more information to the meaning of your Mayan astrology sign.

The numbers that accompany the day sign have not had as much attention paid to them as the nature of the day sign itself. Some of the Mayan calendar scholars and authors of Mayan astrology books have left the numbers out of their books completely.

In working with the astrology in different ways, such as doing Mayan astrology Tree of Life chart readings and using the Mayan Day Keeper system of divination, I have come to see how the numbers play important roles in different aspects of the Mayan astrology system. The numbers make a great difference in working with these advanced Mayan practices. In this book, I will only be discussing the way the numbers are used to find your Mayan astrology sign.

In his book Jaguar Wisdom, Kenneth Johnson relates the belief of the Maya that feel that the lower numbers, 2-5, carry less than the full energy of the day sign. He expressed the idea that the Maya feel 6-9 were the balanced numbers that integrated the number with the day sign in a harmonious way. They feel that the higher numbers, 10-13 have too much energy of the day sign to be in balance.

It is my perspective that the number that accompanies your day sign is an importance influence that needs to be considered as part of your nature. The number joins with the day sign to give more definition to the personality of the day sign.

I like to compare the number to the concept of the moon in Western astrology. In the same way that the sun and moon are central to a Western astrology chart, the day sign and number blend together like the sun and moon in a Western astrology chart. These two influences combine to create your unique personality. The same is true in Mayan astrology with the day sign and number.

I have found through my experience working with individuals that people born with the higher numbers are very strong representations of their day sign. I have found that the higher numbers are very high energy. Higher numbers often take their essence out into the world in a big way. Many very successful, famous people have high numbers. Diana Ross is a 13 Reed, Lucille Ball was a 13 Road, Abraham Lincoln a 12 Night, Humphrey Bogart a 12 Eagle, Benjamin Franklin was a 13 Earth and "The Sleeping Prophet" Edgar Cayce was a 13 Jaguar. The high numbers seem to be able to push the day sign out into the world to gain prominence or infamy. Ian was a 12 Sun and Sigmund Freud was a 10 Reed

Those who are born with the number one are the purist representation of the day sign. They represent the pure essence of the day sign because they are not influenced by other day signs. They have not been born into a week ruled by another day sign. I will discuss this concept more when we get to the Mayan week.

NUMBER ONE
Unity, Assertive, Intention, Beginnings

Those born with the number one are good at starting projects. Ones are able to gather the energy that they need to create. Ones are usually in touch with creative energy in some way. They are independent and do not like to take advice from others. Ones have their own guidance system. They have very strong convictions and will often devote themselves to a cause that may be the focus of the lives. They do not like to follow daily routines and often feel that they are in a rut if they do not have enough variety in their lives. These people are always open to try what is new. Ones like a challenge and will work hard to accomplish their goals.

The one personality can be aggressive and even domineering. They usually have very strong opinions. They have a lot of inner physical and emotional strength to call upon when there is a crisis in their lives. Even though they may be hard to get along with sometimes, they can be loyal friends and good partners. They can be very stable, yet very unique characters.

NUMBER TWO
Duality, Polarity, Mystery, Charismatic

Two people are often mysterious. They are attuned to the rhythms of the earth. Twos seem to draw people to them. It is very important for two people to follow their instincts. They have a very profound inner guidance system. Two people are very charismatic. They are open and friendly. They are usually very loving and enjoy being in relationships. They attract partnership. Finding the balance in relationship is vital for two people.

Two people also have a very strong psychic or spiritual side. Many have powerful visions. Duality is a lifelong struggle for two people. They sometimes find it hard to walk in the world that we know as the earth plane and also be aware of the world of spirit. When they are able to balance all the aspects of their lives, they can achieve greatness.

NUMBER THREE
Action, Artistic, Movement, Activation

If you are born with the number three, you will always be on the move, in some way or other. Threes like to initiate change and variety. Three people have a great sense of rhythm. They usually enjoy expressing themselves through movement. Dance and music are a big part of a three person's life. Art is another area that threes excel in. They like to work in seclusion, but what they create is for the whole world. Their living space is very important to them, and they may have more than one place that they call home. Threes will usually reside in a aesthetically pleasing place or home.

Three people need to be able to express themselves freely. When they do this it clears their energy fields and helps them to focus and be productive. The struggle for inner peace is always a big concern for three people. They often are plagued with doubt and uncertainty. They may enjoy taking risks and other types of adventures. They often try to help others find balance and harmony.

NUMBER FOUR
Structure, Foundation, Stability

In the way that threes are always moving, the four people are always looking for and appreciating foundation and stability. A four person will work tirelessly to create roots or a home base. They need to have a safe place to land where they feel secure and protected. Those born under the number 4 are practical and in touch with reality. These people are very good at following routines and plans. They are humble in nature. They do not like to lead, but will be an avid supporter of a situation they feel is structured and has a firm foundation. Once they make their mind up, it is hard for them to see other perspectives. They have a great deal of inner strength that they can call upon to keep their world in balance.

NUMBER FIVE
Intelligent, Centers, Gathers, Empowers

Those with five energy can be very persuasive and inspiring to others. Five people are very intelligent. They love to question what they see around them. They enjoy gathering information and organizing it into something productive. They are aware of that saying "Knowledge is Power".

Five people are usually very organized. The five born also have a desire to investigate many areas of life. They love mystery and intrigue.

They love to oversee projects to make sure they are done correctly. Fives also will be the first to question a plan or situation that they feel is not being handled properly. If you are involved with a five person, let them take charge. You will be happier that way. They are very competent and usually rise to the top of any organization or group. They are hard workers and often ahead of their time. They will be the first to reach their monthly quota or other goal. They make powerful administrators. Fives can also be a bit impulsive, so sometimes they need to be kept on track to achieve their desires.

NUMBER SIX
Responsive, Creates flow

If you are a six person, then you know that beginnings and endings are part of life. You do not fight changes, but allow yourself to work with them. Most six people are very practical and like life to be structured in terms of concrete situations. Six people can be good negotiators. A six personality is always interested in making whatever is going on in their life better. They are responsive to the needs of others and will usually try to find a solution that will work for all concerned. Six people are very dynamic in nature and will attract what is needed in their life to keep their life going smoothly. They like to be helpful to others.

A six person can tend to be critical. They can also suffer from an indulgent nature. They can flow into many situations that they may not really desire and then berate themselves for ending up where they are. It is important for six people not to be too hard on themselves. When their criticism is tempered six people can really focus on concrete achievement.

NUMBER SEVEN
Reflects, Maintains

Seven people are very different from the six people. They are not concerned with the group, but like solitude. They are strong individuals. They like to ponder the mysteries of life by themselves. Sevens have a very spiritual nature. They seem to be in touch with endings and help bring grace to the conclusion of situations. They can be attracted to the dark or the light. They will be the first to question authority. The seven people have a stubborn streak that can be seen when you try to get them to change their minds. Even though the seven nature makes them appear distant and even isolated, they are loyal friends and will stick by a someone they care about through whatever may come.

NUMBER EIGHT
Justice, Balances, Harmonizes

The eight nature is one of structuring and restructuring. Eights are in a continual process of evolving and redefining what already exists. An eight person is always interested in changing boundaries. These people are always attracted to what is new and different. They are the inventors of the world. This applies to spiritual beliefs and practices as well as material ones. They can often play the hero if the need arises.

Eight people love to travel and see what the world is like in other places and with other perspectives. You will not get set in your ways if you are involved with an 8. You will never be bored either! They can be volatile and changeable. They may get annoyed at you if you are not flexible.

NUMBER NINE
Patience, Perseverance, Completion

Those born under the number nine are forceful and have very deep beliefs. They are able to persevere until a project is done. Nine people are great with details. They like to feel that whatever they are working on has a higher purpose or is working for the greater good. Nine people can be moody and can be overtaken by depression. This creates a paradox for them. They want to complete their work, but feel that everything is pointless when the gloom sets in.

The number nine is also associated with patience. This is because nine people are all about getting to the finish line of whatever is important to them at the time. When they are in the right frame of mind, a nine person will keep going until the goal is achieved. This quality makes nine people very good at creating prosperity.

NUMBER TEN
Manifestation, Refinement, Challenges

This is the number of manifestation. Ten people like to take what is raw and unrefined and bring it into the world. Those born under the number ten are able to create with whatever is around to make something valuable and beautiful emerge. When a ten person has direction and focus, they will attract what is necessary to turn their thoughts and visions into reality. They are very vulnerable and can get off track when emotions get out of balance.

Whatever a ten creates must have a strong foundation in order to be successful. If ten people lose sight of their goal or try to do too many things at one time, it will dissipate their creative energy and they will not be able to manifest their dreams. Ten people are usually very responsible, but they do have a tendency to accrue debts. Their drive to manifest can often disregard the means that they use to birth their ideas. Tens need to be mindful that the end does not always justify the means. If they focus on their goals and are in harmony with the steps that are needed to get them there, they will manifest their visions.

NUMBER ELEVEN
Resolution, Facilitates change

Eleven people have the ability to strip away what no longer serves so that they can move forward into new creation. Eleven people are really good at seeing what may be useless at this present time and releasing it. The nature of eleven people is to be a bit aloof. This can be difficult when an eleven person is in a relationship. They constantly clear away the old within themselves. They help others to release what is hindering them. Being true to oneself is very important for an eleven person. They are always looking for balance for themselves and where they are in the world. They have an innate desire to balance what has been out of whack. Many eleven people are interested in healing. They may be physical or emotional healers. They have a lot of potential, but may lack the direction to see projects to the end. Some elevens will feel lost, and may have trouble staying on their set course of action.

Creativity is an important part of the eleven make up. When they pace themselves, they can bring many creative endeavors to the world. Eleven people often are very successful when they focus on overcoming challenges that come into their lives and hone their creative potentials.

NUMBER TWELVE
Understanding, Retrospection, Summary

This number signifies endings and new beginnings. For this reason those with the twelve energy have a certain melancholy about them. Even though they seem to be in touch with endings, twelve people are interested in activation of change and regeneration. These people will always help others set a new course. Ian was a twelve person. During the time that we were together, he was always reinventing himself and starting new directions. He was a virtual fountain of dreams that were continually bubbling up to the surface of his mind. The twelve has the ability to save what was useful from the old and incorporate it in to a new beginning. For this reason, twelve people make good counselors. They can help people pick up the pieces of their lives that have been shattered and start anew. They have abundant energy for reaching goals and recreating life experience.

Twelve people can also get in trouble from bragging. I saw that happen a lot when I was with Ian. They are enchanted with the past. This is why Ian was so taken with the Maya. When a twelve person is able to stick to a project and complete it, they can achieve a great deal. Completing projects will get them the acknowledgement and praise for a job well done that they desire.

NUMBER THIRTEEN
Ascension, Authority, Intensity, Completion

The number thirteen, to the Maya, was a very powerful number. It represented going to the highest level of accomplishment. Those born with the number thirteen will be very good at tying up loose ends, making sure all the details of a project are in order. Thirteen people are always interested in improving upon what they have created. Thirteen is at that point of getting ready to jump into the void to start a new cycle or project. Thirteen often has their feet in both worlds. They are at home in the void, for they know that the void is that from which manifestation begins. They can sense new trends before they manifest in the world.

Thirteen people are often psychics or artists. A thirteen person will always have a lot of intense experiences that they will either create or the people in their life will create for them. Unexpected change is always part of a thirteen person's life. For a thirteen person to be happy, they need to realize that change is a constant in their lives. They will be pleased with their lives if they can be flexible and allow new situations in. Thirteen is always standing on the precipice of any area of life, ready to jump off into a new creation, or take it something already created to the next level.

THE ENERGIES OF THE DIRECTIONS

This chapter will expound upon the basic nature of the four directions and the role they play in Mayan calendar astrology. Like most native cultures of the Americas, the Mayan sacred calendar, the Tzolkin, integrates the concept of the four directions in its foundation. Native American indigenous cultures have a color assigned to each of the four directions. It seems that each Native American tribe usually has their own take on which color represents which direction. I am honoring the information that Ian received from the shaman with whom he worked. It is my understanding that the color assigned to each direction on the chart is the same as the colors the Kiche' Maya use. From the research that I have done I can say that the majority of Maya, including the Yucatec Maya, also adhere to these same colors for the directions.

EAST/RED/FIRE

This direction is represented by the color red. This stands for the colors of the sunrise. It is the place where the day begins, so red represents initiation of activity. The direction of the East is where galactic light energy is expressed through emotions, passions, and activity. Ian and I used red to represent beginnings and birthing of new projects. It is the start of new experiences or journeys. The day signs that are ruled by the East are energizing, stimulating and full of movement and vigor. The eastern signs are brimming over with energy, passion and intensity that will be expressed in the physical, mental or emotional arenas of life. The day signs of the East are Crocodile, Serpent, Offering, Reed and Earth. Crocodile, Serpent and Offering express passions in a down to earth fashion. Reed and Earth express passions with their thoughts and ideals.

NORTH/WHITE/AIR

This direction usually represents knowledge that comes with experience. This theme of knowledge coming from the North is why many Native American traditions feel that their departed relatives and wise elders reside in the North. The wise ones will come to the service of mankind, like a helpful grandfather or grandmother, when they are asked for guidance. Due to the insight and perception the elders both alive and dead can communicate, the North is believed to be the source of mental activity and communication. Therefore the mind and thought that does travel through the air have become the qualities that are associated with the direction of the north. Four of the 5 day signs from the North communicate spiritual information. Wind communicates on the surface of the earth. Dog, Transformer and Jaguar are conduits for communication to the underworld. Flint carries the energy of the priest or priestess through which galactic light energy speaks and brings communications from the center of the galaxy to humanity. The day signs that are under the sway of the direction of the North are usually very mental, analytical and communicative.

WEST/BLUE/WATER

This direction has been assigned the color blue. The Kiche' Maya sometimes use the color black for the West as well. Due to the fact that the West is where the sun sets for the day, the West is associated with endings. At the time of death, many native cultures believe that the soul is thought to return to the realm of the underworld in the West.

The direction of the West is associated with water. Many primitive societies understood the fluid, symbolic nature of the subconscious. I feel that is why water is associated with the subconscious and the West. This association of water with the direction of the West also comes from the awareness that the deep darkness of the ocean hides what is below the surface. Ancient spiritual knowledge relates that the psyche, the human sub conscious, also hides much of each person's nature and experiences.

Those day signs that are linked with the West usually have a strong connection to the subconscious and imagery. It is from this connection that galactic light energy communicates through symbols and other creative manifestations.

Most indigenous cultures have a great understanding of what the Maya call the underworld. The subconscious or underworld is where illness starts and healing takes place. Even though the Maya practiced human sacrifice and were primitive in many ways they also understood the commanding role that the sub conscious plays in the life of every person. Those born into the day signs of the West are able to go through the doorway of the subconscious to express the power of the psyche.

Galactic light energy works through the day signs ruled by the West by having them be the conduit to the hidden parts of humanity.

The West ruled day signs also have a strong connection to healing and intuitive abilities. The day signs that are ruled by the west are Night, Deer, Monkey, Eagle and Storm. Night and Storm have the strongest intuitive abilities of the West ruled day signs. Monkey and Deer and Storm express this connection to the intuitive through creativity and art. Eagle and Night can see the future through their connection to the sub conscious.

SOUTH/YELLOW/EARTH

This direction is thought, by many tribes throughout the world, to represent physical endurance and focus on material life. In many Native American societies, the South typifies the playful, childlike qualities of humans and all other creatures. The South is connected with the body and the physical aspects of life. Therefore, the South represents the concept of a child starting out on their road of life, looking for understanding and exploring life through experiences that involve the five senses of the body. Many of the day signs that are connected to the South have strong connections to the physical body and daily life.

The association of the body with fertility plays a key role in the energy of the South. The day sign ruled by the South have a major theme of growth, death and rebirth woven within them. Galactic light energy works through those linked to the South by having them manifest spiritual energy in a tangible, material way. The day signs of the South are Seed, Star, Road, Wisdom and Sun. Seed and Road are concerned with manifestation on the material level. Star works with moving and regulating manifestation. Wisdom is concerned with cleansing and purification of the physical and releasing or transforming what is not immortal from the world. Sun is concerned with being the ruler and example to others, the top of the pyramid, and the pinnacle of what humanity can be.

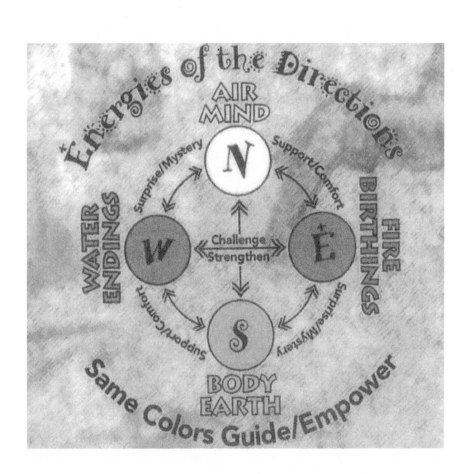

THE EMPOWERING, NURTURING, SURPRISING AND CHALLENGING INTERACTION OF THE DAY SIGNS

Apart from the directions assisting an individual in learning more about their personal nature, the Maya have used them in their astrology to bring another dimension to the interaction of the day signs and with the energy of the day. The order of the day signs are very important. The same order, starting with Crocodile, has been discussed in many of the surviving texts. When you look at the **TZOLKIN chart** you will notice that the day signs alternate. Every fourth day a different color or direction dominates for a 24 hour period, from dawn to dawn. Please refer to the **ENERGIES OF THE DIRECTIONS chart** while you are ingesting the following information. It will make it much easier to follow.

Every fourth day, a different direction has authority over the present day. When the direction of the day sign of the present day is the same as the direction or color of your day sign, it is an EMPOWERING day for you. That is because the direction of your personal day sign is with the most harmonious match of any of the four directions. It is like doubling your energy, so naturally it is known as a day that amplifies your personal power. To use the terminology of Western astrology, the empowering days are like conjunctions. These types of conjunctions are usually beneficial to the empowered day sign.

The SUPPORT days are similar to the way a trine works in Western astrology. They are very positive or helpful days, similar to the empowering days. On support days energies flow smoothly and you will find, if you choose to take note of your experiences on support days, that they will be enjoyable and nurturing for you. You will get the help you need or feel comforted.

Every day sign has a CHALLENGE day. This can be thought of as the opposition of Western astrology. As you can see from looking at the chart, your personal challenge day is the direction that is opposite your direction. This can be the most difficult of the four days. Ian and I decided to call it strengthening as well as challenging. This is because, as I explained to him about Western astrology, an opposition can force you to act and deal with a challenge or stagnant situation. We all know that dealing with our challenges will help us grow in many ways, even if it is not always a fun experience.

The last type of day that you will experience is the MYSTERY/SURPRISE day. This type of day could be likened to a type of aspect in Western astrology called a square. Even though squares in Western astrology are usually associated with difficulty, the surprise/mystery day for you on the Tzolkin can be either a happy or not so happy surprise. I have noticed as I have kept track of the impact of these days, that my mystery/surprise day can be a surprise like unexpected money or good events happening or it can be a surprise bill that you thought was going to be much less.

The key word here is mystery. It accounts for that unexplained energy that manifests in our lives. One way to think of the mystery/surprise day or week is to borrow the concept of Karma. Positive or negative repercussions can come back to you for the thoughts and actions you have sent out to the planet on mystery/surprise days. I like to think of the mystery/surprise day as being akin to that idea of what you get in your stocking from Santa Claus at Christmas. Santa (the Universe/Powers that Be) knows what you should have. You will get the sweet treat or the lump of coal, depending upon your past actions and the way this energy needs to be expressed. The mystery/surprise day acknowledges that the there is an energy that flows through all of creation. This energy impacts you in ways that your conscious mind is not capable of understanding while encased in the limiting confines of the human form.

COMPATIBILITY

Please read the next four paragraphs to grasp the concepts behind compatibility in the Mayan astrology system. This will help you understand the relationships of **empowerment, support, challenge and mystery** in the interactions of the day signs with each other.

This concept is a major part of Western astrology as well as Mayan astrology. Compatibility in the Mayan system, like all aspects of this system, is very simple. Compatibility is based on the way the directions of each day sign interact. As I have indicated in the previous chapter, compatibility is based on the interaction of directions with each other. In the same way that you have a empowering, supportive, challenging and mystery days, you will also have that type of relationship with other day signs.

If your day sign is ruled by the **South**, like **Seed, Star, Road, Wisdom** and **Sun**, you will have an **empowering relationship** with day signs ruled by the **same direction**. These day signs help you strengthen you and bring out your highest potential. These are usually productive relationships. These people will bring out the best in you and help you to achieve your goals.

As a day sign ruled by the **South,** you will find that your **comfort and support relationships** happen with **Night, Deer, Monkey, Eagle and Storm** are comfort/support relationships because they are your nurturing and support relationships. Your **challenging** partners will come from the **North: Wind, Transformer, Dog, Jaguar and Flint**. These people will bring out your challenges, but they will also help you to grow and strengthen yourself.

The most interesting relationships for the **South** will be found with the **mystery/surprise** relationships with **Crocodile, Serpent, Offering, Reed and Earth.** These people will keep you guessing and you will have to be on your toes. This may be successful for you or may not. There may just be too much disparity in your connection to make it last. Or you may be like fire and ice, but somehow it will work for you. That is the mystery of this connection.

The **day signs from the North,** namely **Wind, Transformer, Dog, Jaguar** and **Flint** will find **empowerment** with their same direction. Your **support** signs are **Crocodile, Serpent, Offering, Reed and Earth.** The **challenging** signs for **North** day signs are **Seed, Star, Road, Wisdom** and **Sun.** Your **mystery/surprise** signs are **Night, Deer, Monkey, Eagle and Storm.**

The day signs ruled by the **East, Crocodile, Serpent, Offering, Reed and Earth,** will **empower** by each other. Your signs of **support** are **Wind, Transformer, Dog, Jaguar and Flint.** The **challenges** come from the **West** and the day signs of **Night, Deer, Monkey, Eagle and Storm.** Your greatest **surprises** will come from the **South** in the form of the day signs **Seed, Star, road, Wisdom and Sun.**

Those born into the direction of the **West,** namely **Night, Deer, Monkey, Eagle and Storm** will **empower** each other. Your **support** team is made up of the **Southern** day sign of **Seed, Star, Road, Wisdom and Sun. Challenges** will come from the **East** and **the Crocodile, Serpent, Offering, Reed and Earth** day signs. Life's **mysteries** will come from the **North** and the day signs of **Wind, Transformer, Dog, Jaguar and Flint.**

There are a few aspects that will influence relationships. Often, as with Ian and I, challenging relationships will be powerful connections. These relationships will usually test you to go beyond your comfort zone. Many great achievements can come about from this type of union.

The other interesting type of connection is the mystery/surprise connection. These relationships can give you great ecstasy or incredible trauma. These connections cannot be categorized as easy or difficult. They may involve some type of past life connection that needs to have closure or healing in order to be released. They may bring the bliss of a relationship from another life into your awareness. In any event, there are powerful reasons why the mystery/surprise connection manifests in your life.

THE MAYAN WEEK AND ITS INFLUENCE ON THE DAY SIGNS

The concept of the Mayan week in the Tzolkin is a period of 13 days. There are 20 Mayan weeks in the Tzolkin. Each of the day signs has their own Mayan Week. To use a term from Western astrology **each day sign is the ruler of its own Mayan week.** This means that the day sign that is the number one for that 13 day period influences the day signs that are within its week .During each of the 20 weeks in the Tzolkin, a different day sign gets a chance to shine forth its brightness. This influence is present in the Mayan week into which you were born, and also during the present week of each Tzolkin "year" or current round.

The Mayan week that you are born into does have an impression upon your nature. Along with your day sign and number, the Mayan week does have an impact upon you. I like to think of the influence of the ruling day sign of each Mayan week as a pale watercolor wash that goes over a painting and has a subtle effect upon the color of the painting.

To use examples with the definitions of Western astrology, the Mayan day sign can be compared to your sun sign, the number to the influence of the moon and the number one of your Mayan week is like the rising sign. Even though this is an oversimplified representation, it will give you some basis for comparison. In Western astrology, the sun sign, moon and rising sign have the strongest impact in the birth chart. In Mayan astrology, the day sign, number and ruler of the Mayan week you are born in come together in much the same way to create a trinity of influence upon you.

It has been said by some Mayan scholars that the power of the day sign is doubled when their day sign is the number one. This can be said to be true because the number one day signs are not influenced by the energy or another day sign.

For example, my day sign is Flint and my number is one. Therefore I carry the doubled power of Flint. I will have to say that I am certainly making a great effort to bring the truth, as I know it, about the Maya and Mayan astrology to the public. This is a primary, driving force for Flints.

What this translates to for those born into day signs during a One Flint week is that they will also have a desire to bring the truth to light. They may also have healing ability and excel in communication fields even though their day sign is not known for that inclination.

In order to find the **ruler of your Mayan week**, if you are not a number one, first **find your Mayan day sign on the Tzolkin chart**. Then just **go back through the Tzolkin chart until you come to the number one**. If you are a 13 Serpent, follow the numbers back until you come to one Reed. I will go into brief descriptions about the nature of each Mayan week and how each day sign is influenced by its Mayan birthday week.

ONE CROCODILE
THE PRIMAL MOTHER

The focus of the Crocodile day sign is home and family. It is a day sign that is very protective of the loved ones. Jealousy and domination can be part of the protective feelings of the Crocodile. This day sign is very emotional, creative and good at starting projects.

Day signs effected: 2 Wind, 3 Night, 4 Seed, 5 serpent,6 Transformer, 7 Deer, 8 Star,9 Offering, 10 Dog, 11 Monkey, 12 Road, 13 Reed.

TWO WIND

The influence of the Crocodile day sign can have a very positive effect on a 2 Wind person. It can bring about roots and stability for the Wind person. The 2 Wind person can be very successful in having a lasting relationship and family with the Crocodile influence. Crocodile is a nurturing sign for Wind, so the influence will be positive.

Rod Sterling, the creator of the Twilight Zone, was a 2 Wind who was able to bring awareness of life on other frequencies and dimensions to the mind of humanity.

THREE NIGHT

The Crocodile day sign can enhance the desire of Night people for friends and family. With the Crocodile influence, Night people can come out of their caves and bring the warmth and passion that is needed to maintain a close circle of people in one's life. The 3 Night person will be more grounded and in tune with family life. Crocodile is a challenging/strengthening influence for Night, so Night may have struggles in manifesting the prosperity they desire for their family. Night people may also go through a conflict about family life vs. the quiet cave time.

FOUR SEED

The already strong energy of fertility and creation for the Seed day sign will be enhanced with the Crocodile essence. It will help the Seed person balance their desire for family life with their desire to be free and to express their sexuality. Crocodile is in a mystery/surprise relationship to Seed. The Seed person can achieve their goals if they flow with the easy going pace of the Crocodile and let situations unfold naturally.

FIVE SERPENT

This is a very strong position for this Serpent day sign. If you are born into this placement you will be empowered by the Crocodile energy. This will tend to make this Serpent more of a home body and think about offspring, if this Serpent wishes to have children. The thing to watch out for here is the explosive temper. The potential to react in a strong and even violent manner will be squared. Keep this in mind when you are dealing with others. A lot of devotees or friends will be under the sway of the Serpent, so those who are born under this day sign need perspective to be in integrity and not take advantage of its hypnotic potential. The empowering energy of Crocodile can make this day sign seem larger than life. Marilyn Monroe was a 5 Serpent who perhaps did not know the power of her effect upon others.

SIX TRANSFORMER

The influence of Crocodile is also very harmonious for this day sign as its natural interest in family and community will be amplified. The Crocodile influence may cause this day sign to be more aggressive in working for friends and family. It may make this day sign a bit of a control freak in order to get the Transformer goals accomplished. This day sign may also have a bit of a temper that is part of the Crocodile nature. With the supportive influence of Crocodile, this day sign will be able to create a secure life for the ones they love.

SEVEN DEER

The Deer day sign always has a conflict between family and freedom. With this Crocodile wash, Deer may find it even more of a challenge to create a family structure. This day sign may even have a great fear of getting close to people. This will strengthen them if they are able to work with this challenge. Then they can create a close circle of family or friends that will support them in their need to roam the world, yet still give them someplace to call home. The usually gentle Deer also needs to watch their temper and not be too opinionated. Kurt Vonnegut and Allen Ginsberg are two 7 Deers who were able to create their own world while sharing the observations of life. Both men have their strong circle of followers.

EIGHT STAR

The influence of Crocodile can make this day sign very competitive. There is also a tendency to manifest the dominating tendency of the Crocodile. When this tendency is used positively, these Star people can be great leaders and administrators. The Star person may go with their gut more than their intellect, which is the Crocodile mode of functioning. They will most likely put a lot of their creativity to use in creating an interesting home and circle of friends and family.

NINE OFFERING

The power of the Crocodile emotions will run strong within this day sign, which is already very emotional. This may translate into very irrational or controversial actions. These unusual actions can manifest as charisma that propels Offering people into leadership roles with those that are taken with them. Indira Ghandi had this charismatic frequency that gave her the leadership of India at a very crucial time in that nation's history. This is an empowering placement for the Offering person, and they can reach great heights in life.

TEN DOG

This position of the Dog in the Crocodile week will strengthen Dog's desire for family and community. They can become very focused on parenting and nurturing their family. The energy of Crocodile is a harmonious one for the Dog, and their connection to their family will be a major part of their lives. The dominating aspect of Crocodile may come into play with Dog in this position. The loyalty that Dog feels for their loved ones or whoever they feel comes within their territorial parameters may translate into Crocodile's desire to have things their way.

ELEVEN MONKEY

The familial nature of Crocodile may create a conflict within the Monkey nature. This placement creates a need to be focused on domestic structure. The Crocodile desire to blossom within the home and family structure is in opposition to the freewheeling nature of the Monkey. The Monkey person will have to work to either live with a dominating family structure that they may be born into, or will be very possessive of the family they create. Their home will always be beautiful, with a lot of creativity about. It is easy to see the Monkey influence in Edgar Rice Burroughs, the creator of Tarzan, the Ape Man. Tarzan was a family man who swung around in the trees a lot but always came back to Jane.

TWELVE ROAD

Even though Crocodile has the influence of mystery or surprise for this day sign, the Crocodile emphasis for the Road day sign gives them an even stronger inclination to be successful for those that they consider their family. The Road person may either have some unexpected positive surprises or disappoints that result from Road's total focus and dedication to their family. Jeff Bridges, the son of Lloyd Bridges, the television actor, has received a lot of benefit from starting his acting career from the springboard of a family that was involved in the acting profession.

THIRTEEN REED

The tendency to dominate others, which is part of the Crocodile nature, can become very strong within 13 Reed people. It also gives their emotions and charisma even greater force than is usual for the Reed person. This can be seen in the life of 13 Reed Diana Ross. She definitely broke new ground for the black entertainer of her day. This position of Reed can bring out the desire to bring their passion to the world. If these Reed people get into leadership roles, it will probably have some domestic or family focal point.

ONE JAGUAR
CONDUIT TO THE UNDERWORLD

The Jaguar is a day sign that likes to be secretive or work behind the scenes. They rarely reveal what they are thinking to others. The stealth of the Jaguar also puts them in touch with many areas of life that many feel are mysterious: the subconscious. Their flair for material manifestation may also benefit those born into their week. The day signs of this week are 2 Eagle, 3 Wisdom, 4 Earth, 5 Flint, 6 Storm, 7 Sun, 8 Crocodile, 9 Wind, 10 Night, 11 Seed, 12 Serpent and 13 Transformer.

TWO EAGLE

This placement can be a contrast to the basic nature of the Eagle, which is to be up in the air and highly visible. The Eagle finds itself in unfamiliar territory that goes along with the mystery and surprise of the relationship of Jaguar and Eagle. The Eagle may become withdrawn and not in touch with their natural ability as a leader. These Eagles may be very shy and private, which is part of the Jaguar make-up. Events of surprise will be needed to shock the Eagle into attuning to their true nature.

Henry David Thoreau was one such Eagle, who sought the solitude of Nature. Being close to the earth is another trait of the Jaguar. The mental ability of the air element can be seen in his incredible aptitude to communicate.

THREE WISDOM

The already serious nature of Wisdom is heightened by the need of the Jaguar to be hidden and behind the scenes. This combination enhances the Wisdom's desire to bring the riches of the earth into the upper world for financial abundance and prosperity. These Wisdoms will have a strong connection to the cleansing and healing the earth and may be involved in environmental causes. This is a challenge position for Wisdom, so they may have many struggles to overcome to reach their goals. The dedication of the wisdom nature will help them achieve their desires, even against many challenges.

FOUR EARTH

The Jaguar influence can be very calming to the Earth day sign. The sharp Earth mind that is always going, can find sanctuary in the calm recesses of the sub conscious. This placement can also be very good for the Earth person in that they will tend to dig deeper into the subjects that they find interesting, instead of jumping from one to the other. The comfort and support that the Jaguar gives to the Earth person can be very helpful to them as they seek to balance the seemingly opposite tendencies of these two day signs. This meeting of opposites, the conscious mind and the sensitivity to the subconscious came together very favorably for 4 Earth politician and president of the United States, Theodore Roosevelt. The Jaguar connection to the earth was very apparent in Theodore Roosevelt's love of nature and his accomplishments.

FIVE FLINT

The mental focus of the Flint person can be softened by the influence of the Jaguar. The Flint person is always seeking the truth or meaning under what is hidden. With the help of the Jaguar, the Flint person can connect with the subtle yet powerful flow of the sub conscious. This will help the Flint person to seek out knowledge of the spiritual, psychic or energy healing realms to add to their collection of tools that they use to help others. This is an empowering placement for the Flint person. This means that they will be successful in all that they attempt to do as long as they maintain the balance between the sub conscious and the intellect.

This Flint person may be a bit reclusive, but they will most likely make discoveries about themselves and their lives that will help them utilize their full potential.

SIX STORM

The Storm personality is one that may be bewildered by the Jaguar impact upon their lives. This is because the Jaguar is a mystery/surprise relationship for the Storm person. The nature of the Jaguar is to hide, so the naturally gregarious Storm person may be a bit reclusive. Surprise will be a constant in the life of this Storm person. This day sign is naturally in touch with the sub conscious, being that the ruling direction is the West, where the subconscious resides. Even though Storm people can do well in careers where communication is necessary, the Jaguar influence may cause this Storm person to do work that may be secretive in nature. Pete Seeger is person who has the Jaguar ability to communicate with the emotional connection of Storm.

SEVEN SUN

This day sign is able to use the connection that the Jaguar brings to explore their inner nature. They may use their artistic creativity to understand the human condition. Since Sun is a day sign of the Mayan rulers, Sun is often very noble and unable to connect with real people. The impact of the Jaguar on Sun is able to bring this lofty day sign down to earth and even into their inner nature. Jaguar is in a challenging relationship with Sun. Therefore the self discovery and connection to the real world may be difficult to the Sun person, but it will bring balance and a well rounded personality in the end. This may make it easier for the Sun person to have relationships that can last and be happy.

EIGHT CROCODILE

Even though the Jaguar is in a comfort and support relationship to the emotional Crocodile, they really have opposite natures that need to come into balance. The Crocodile wants to be surrounded by friends and family who know everything about them. The Jaguar wants to be private and secretive.

This dance of balance can be seen in the life and career of an 8 Crocodile, Johnny Cash. His strong connection to family that is evidenced in his relationship with June, his wife, helped him to succeed in his career.

His tendency to indulge in addictions, which can be a tendency within the Jaguar, almost shattered all that he worked for in his career and marriage. He was able to find balance and was able to bring his passion for Country music to great heights.

NINE WIND

The energy of Jaguar is empowering to this day sign that is also from the direction of the North. The grounded nature of the Jaguar is able to help the 9 Wind people from being scattered and ineffective. This powerful combination can be seen in the life of Elizabeth Taylor. Even though she was a bit fickle and changeable with husbands, which is a quality of the Wind, she was grounded enough to be able to make use of her love of acting and communication and become a very famous and successful woman.

Another 9 Wind person, Larry Flint, also made use of his desire to communicate with his pornography empire. The Jaguar gave him the stability and the means to derive riches from his interests.

TEN NIGHT

Here the secretive nature of the Jaguar only compounds the Night person's desire to be reclusive. The Jaguar can help the Night person attain their goals of financial security. As long as the Night person is true to themselves and follow their dreams, they can be very successful.

Unusual or unexpected success happens because the Night person is in a mystery and surprise relationship with the Jaguar energy. Literally anything can happen and this day sign can definitely break new ground. The career of Dan Rather, the news reporter, was built on reporting shocking, unexpected events. The JFK assignation and Richard Nixon's Watergate were just two of the shocking world class events that that brought Dan Rather to prominence in his field.

ELEVEN SEED

The day sign of Jaguar is in opposition to the Seed day sign. This tends to put a damper on the Seed's natural tendency to be gregarious and to network. This means that it may be challenging for the Seed person to create the net of connections that is a basic aspect of their nature. It will be challenging for the Seed person to let their light shine, especially when the Jaguar likes to slink around in the dark.

Once the Seed person comes to terms with this aspect of their personality and works with it, they can see a deeper side of life. These trials will only strengthen the Seed person and help them to achieve the fortitude to let their true nature shine forth.

TWELVE SERPENT

The Jaguar is in a supportive relationship with the Serpent. This helps the Serpent to have even greater hypnotic sway over people. It also helps the Serpent to utilize their mental abilities that often get lost when a Serpent is born in a week ruled by another day sign from the East. The high number may produce a persuasive, dynamic personality.

Both the Jaguar and the Serpent have a strong connection to the earth, earth magic and gemstones. With the help of the Jaguar, the Serpent can use these tendencies to become a healer with the help of the herbs, crystals and the energy of the earth. The Serpent person may also have a strong connection to doing soul retrieval work, which takes place in the familiar Jaguar territory of the underworld. The Jaguar will help the Serpent achieve the material prosperity to manifest their creative and political goals.

THIRTEEN TRANSFORMER

Here the power of these two day signs can combine to give this placement of Transformer powerful psychic and creative abilities. Jaguar and Transformer are two of the day signs that are often involved in some type of spiritual or shamanic practices. The Maya feel that these day signs are able to go to the underworld for the healing of others. This empowering connection can help Transformer achieve its potential to be financially abundant in this type of career.

Even though Transformer is very community oriented, this placement may make this day sign withdrawn. This may be necessary for the height of their nature as a shaman or healer to emerge.

ONE DEER
THE ETERNAL WANDERER

Perhaps the central issue for the Deer nature is the conflict between freedom and family commitment. One aspect of the Deer wants to be free to roam the world. Yet there is another aspect of the Deer nature that wants to have the comfort and security of home and family or group consciousness. This causes the influence of the Deer to create this conflict within the day signs over which it has sway. For Deer as well as the day signs born in this week, it is important to find a way to satisfy these two opposing instincts and create a unique life style that works these individuals.

The day signs born into this week are 2 Star, 3 Offering, 4 Dog, 5 Monkey, 6 Road, 7 Reed, 8 Jaguar, 9 Eagle, 10 Wisdom, 11 Earth, 12 Flint and 13 Storm.

TWO STAR

The influence of the Deer week on the Star person is a positive one, since Deer is a supportive day sign for the Star person. Even so, the desire to be free and explore new ideas can get the Star person in trouble if they do not take new experiences in moderation. This was the case with the famous Star person, Elvis Presley. The addictive nature of the Star person definitely got out of hand for The King. The mental genius that is part of the Deer make-up can be enhanced for those Star people born into this placement.

THREE OFFERING

The Deer influence can create a challenge for the Offering person, but may also bring out many positive potentials. This placement can bring accentuate the imagination and psychic abilities. Shirley MacLaine, the actress turned spiritual seeker, brought the psychic area of life into the public eye with her many books about her experiences. Her love of travel and new adventures was helped by the Deer desire to explore.

The Offering person will have to work on focusing this mental stimulus in a positive way. It is important for the 3 Offering person to not let their emotions and imagination run away with them.

FOUR DOG

This position in the Deer week gives this day sign a desire to roam and see the world. This tendency, which is within the Dog day sign, will be enhanced with the Deer influence. Even with this strong need to explore and be free, this placement for Dog also increases the canine's basic tendency to be part of a group or social structure. The surprise relationship with Deer can often cause the Dog person to do a lot of quick dog paddling to get out of unexpected deep water. This Dog may have a pack or close group that travels with them and supports the needs of both Dog and Deer.

FIVE MONKEY

This is an empowering position for the Monkey and this day sign will find that their desire to travel and explore will be amplified. The Monkey's attraction to art and creativity will be enhanced by the Deer's love of beauty and fine art. The conflict that the Deer day sign has in balancing freedom and commitment will be very strong within this placement of Monkey. Carl Reiner, Cab Calloway and Bobby Darin, all in the entertainment industry, have this day sign. The 5 Monkey may have a hard time in committed relationships. They need one that will allow them to express their desire to find new stages upon which to perform.

SIX ROAD

The Road personality will become more social and will find more support than usual with this position in the Deer week. Even though this placement will enhance the Road desire to work for their family, it will also cause this normally stay-at-home day sign to explore more of the world. Liberace, the flamboyant pianist, is an example of a 6 Road that really got out in the world and brought his love of European beauty, and the candelabra, to world consciousness. We all know he had his flair in the costume area!

SEVEN REED

The tendency toward rigidity can become a great conflict for the Reed day sign in this position. The Reed may have problems staying focused enough to get its point across. The Deer's basic desire to be free flowing will challenge the Reed personality's tendency to be fixed and rigid about many matters. In the end, the Reed will come to an expanded point of view. The essence of the Deer will cause the Reed to flow more in life and discover more interesting knowledge.

EIGHT JAGUAR

This position of Jaguar will tend to bring the Jaguar person out of their cave and create a desire for a social network. Nancy Reagan, a famous 8 Jaguar, ruled from the side lines, with her metaphysical focus on Astrology, but definitely got noticed for her influence over the late president of the USA, Ronald Reagan. With this placement, the Jaguar person will probably travel more than most Jaguars. The mystery/surprise influence of the Deer will probably put the Jaguar person into many unexpected situations where the spotlight will shine upon them. It will be a good challenge for the Jaguar to be able to socialize and create a sense of community.

NINE EAGLE

The empowering influence of the Deer nature upon the Eagle will amplify the Eagle's desire to be free and soar to new levels of life experience. These Eagles may even live a type of nomadic life style. Chris Everet, who broke new ground for woman tennis players, was definitely empowered to fulfill the potential of the Eagle and the Deer. On the down side, the problem that the Deer energy has with relationships may also cause this Eagle to have a hard time settling down to focus on relationships.

TEN WISDOM

The Wisdom personality is able to come out of its shell with this placement within the Deer week. With the support of the Deer's gregarious nature, the Wisdom person will have the desire to get out, have some fun and see the world. The Wisdom will also be inclined to study and expand its knowledge due to the Deer's love of beauty and culture.

ELEVEN EARTH

The interest in intellect and rational thought can be enhanced by this placement, even though Earth is in a challenging relationship with the Deer energy. The Deer influence can cause the Earth person, who has a love of rational thought and intellectual stimulation, to look for new arenas of thought to explore. Timothy Leary, the proponent of LSD, definitely broke new ground with his "outside the box" thinking. The Earth person, that is often a home body, may have a tendency to venture out with this placement.

TWELVE FLINT

The Flint's tendency to have problems with close relationships can be amplified with this position in the Deer week. Being that the Deer also has this tendency, the Flint person may find challenges arising in relationships unexpectedly. This position in the Deer week can also give the Flint person the desire to seek out knowledge from around the world. The wanderlust that is natural to the Deer personality may lead the Flint person into some interesting and unexpected experiences and lifestyle choices.

THIRTEEN STORM

The empowering connection between Deer and Storm will help the Storm to explore the world and find many new types of creativity that they choose to imitate or encompass. Since relationship is very important to the Storm person, they may have a nomadic partner who wishes to embrace the desire to travel that will be calling to these Storm people.

ONE SUN
THE WAY OF THE POET KING

Probably the most talented and creative of the day signs, along with Monkey, is the day sign of Sun. This week imbues all those born within it with a variety of talents and high ideals. Practicality and being in touch with reality is the greatest challenge to this day sign.
The day signs that are subjects of this day sign of ancient Mayan kings are 2 Crocodile, 3 Wind, 4 Night, 5 Seed, 6 Serpent, 7 Transformer, 8 Deer, 9 Star, 10 Offering, 11 Dog, 12 Monkey and 13 Road.

TWO CROCODILE

The Crocodiles born into the Sun week will probably feel a calling to use their creativity outside the perimeters of their home and family. The influence of the Sun week will bring out many unexpected opportunities for the Crocodile to be creative and romantic. The Crocodile must learn to be gracious to the people within their lives.

THREE WIND

The desire for love and romance is very strong for this Wind day sign. The tendency of Sun to have idealistic relationships will also be a factor for this Wind day sign. Being that Sun is in the challenge relationship to Wind, this seeker of romance will have many challenges to overcome to find a love relationship that works with their changeable nature. This placement for the Wind day sign will challenge them to create a relationship that can endure many trials.

On the positive side, the creativity of the Sun nature will help the Wind person to express their creativity within mental or communication fields.

FOUR NIGHT

The connection to the creative and spiritual well of the subconscious, which is very strong for those born into the direction of the West, will be enhanced by this position in the Sun week. The supportive connection between Night and Sun will help this normally reclusive day sign bloom in situations that will allow them to express their creative, artistic and spiritual ability.

FIVE SEED

Being born within this week, the Seed person is empowered to enhance their creative ability as well as money making potential. Johnny Carson, the famous talk show host of the Tonight Show, was a Seed who devoted his life to creating a show that brought many unique types of people and fascinating information to the public. This positive placement can bring out the networking potential of the Seed.

SIX SERPENT

This placement of the Serpent brings out their artistic ability due to the influence of the Sun day sign. These Serpents may tend to gravitate toward the entertainment industry. The charisma of the Serpent can come out to the world in unexpected ways that may surprise the Serpent and everyone else. Dance and music are some of the areas of performance in which Serpent will shine froth. This Serpent may be in for some surprises due to the fact that the Sun's influence may cause the Serpent's creative expression to be unappreciated or not readily accepted.

SEVEN TRANSFORMER

High ideals, dedication to a cause and improving the lives of others becomes a life calling for those born into this placement. In this week, the Transformer day sign will make many sacrifices to be of service to others. The astronaut, John Glenn, is an example of a Transformer that put his life on the line to help humanity. Due to the fact that this is a challenging position for the Transformer day sign, it will cause these people to work hard to achieve their goals. The Sun helped John Glenn come out of his cave and go into the world spotlight.

EIGHT DEER

The Deer that has fallen into the Sun week will receive the support of the Sun in achieving their goals. Usually the Deer appreciates beauty. With the help of the Sun, the Deer person will probably get in touch with their own creative expression. The supportive nature of their connection will help the Deer to feel free to pursue their creative and leadership passions.   They will also prosper, or at least become well known for their abilities.

NINE STAR

Due to the empowering influence of the Sun week, the Star person may be someone who appears to be larger than life. This placement will amplify the Star tendency to be famous, and also to have problems with success, power and addictions. This is the case with the famous 60's musician Jimi Hendrix. Even though Star is not noted for it's artistic creativity, with the help of the Sun day sign, this ground breaking entertainer rose to great heights in the music world of his time. His addictive tendencies were also amplified with this position in the Sun week and eventually caused his demise.

TEN OFFERING

This placement in the Sun week gives this already emotional sign unexpected power for presenting their beliefs and creativity. Such was the case with the

Offering person John Lennon, who sky rocketed to fame and fortune with his musical group, The Beatles. The success of his unique emotional perspective on life and his unexpected and untimely death changed the world. His surprising changes in romantic partners also left lasting impressions on our culture. The Sun influence can be seen in Mr. Lennon's idealistic desire to find the perfect romantic partner.

ELEVEN DOG

In this position of challenge, the already friendly Dog may have a desire to experience all life has to offer. This can create loyalty challenges in this position. This Dog has very high ideals of relationship that even they may not be able to live up to. The Dog day sign will probably be a bit self centered and indulgent, which is in line with the nature of the Sun king. The Dog person will probably need to have people helping them instead of putting others first.

TWELVE MONKEY

With the nurturing support of the Sun energy, this day sign and number will be able to reach great heights with their artistic abilities. Performance will be a very strong part of this day sign's life. This propensity for performance combined with the natural leadership abilities of the Sun frequency can be seen in the life a famous 12 Monkey: P.T. Barnum of the Ringling Brothers, Barnum and Bialy Circus. He was definitely a sublime showman as he led performers all over the planet.

THIRTEEN ROAD

Even though Road is one of the humbler day signs, with the empowering energy of the Sun and the number 13, this placement can produce a person that will be very focused on expressing their creative energy. They will more than likely want to be out in front of the camera instead of helping others perform. Lucille Ball was a 13 Road who turned her love of her family and her desire to perform into a world renowned comedy career.

ONE REED
THE DESIRE TO MEDIATE AND ACHIEVE

This day sign is motivated by the desire to constantly improve their lives and to achieve whatever objectives that they feel are important. This can make them good role models, teachers and politicians.
The day signs influenced by the Reed week are 2 Jaguar, 3 Eagle, 4 Wisdom, 5 Earth, 6 Flint, 7 Storm, 8 Sun, 9 Crocodile, 10 Wind, 11 Night, 12 Seed 13 Serpent.

TWO JAGUAR

This position tends to bring the reclusive Jaguar out into the limelight. They may be interested in leadership positions. Even so, the tendency of the Jaguar to amass power and wealth in a hidden way can be seen in the life of a famous 2 Jaguar, Richard Nixon. This placement can bring out the tendency to be manipulating and shrewd. One thing is for sure, the Reed will support the Jaguar in accomplishing their goals.

THREE EAGLE

The desire for competency in the intellectual arenas of life is an influence of the Reed day sign upon the Eagle psyche. This position tends to bring focus for the Eagle in the mental areas of life such as teaching, communication and philosophy. This is a challenging position for the Eagle, so Eagle people may have to struggle or overcome challenges to allow this innate desire to shine forth. The Reed likes to stay put and the Eagle needs freedom, so there may be lifelong conflicts and concessions.

FOUR WISDOM

These people tend to rise to mental heights that are not usually the arena of the Wisdom person. The Reed inclination to achieve goes well with the Wisdom tendency to be serious and regenerative. Being that the Reed has a mystery/surprise relationship with Wisdom; it may be that the Wisdom is rewarded for its tenacious nature in unexpected ways. The Reed will bring many interesting situations into the life of the somber Wisdom person.

FIVE EARTH

The Earth person will greatly benefit from this position in the Reed week, due to the fact that it is an empowering placement for the Earth person. The natural tendency of Earth people to be deep thinkers, teachers and philosophers is given an extra boost by Reed's desire to put thought into action. These Earth people may be very progressive and successful.

SIX FLINT

The Reed proclivity towards high moral and ethical ideals is brought out strongly within this position of Flint. Being that this is a supportive placement for the Flint, it will adapt the high principles of the Reed in career and relationship areas of life. The Reed may help the Flint take a platform to express their ideas and beliefs.

SEVEN STORM

This placement within the Reed week is challenging for the Storm day sign. The Storm person will have to work hard to achieve the high ideals of the Reed influence. The Reed energy will motivate the Storm person to go out into the world and communicate their ideas. These Storm people can excel in writing and speaking. They also have a natural propensity toward teaching and healing. Even though this is a challenging placement, the natures of Reed and Storm can connect in the areas of love of family and commitment.

EIGHT SUN

This day sign is in a mystery and surprise relationship to the ruler of this Mayan week. This can often cause this day sign to act in unexplained ways. Perhaps that is why 8 Sun, Vincent Van Gogh, was inexplicably motivated to cut off his ear .The Reed influence on the Sun day sign can cause them to have unattainable standards of perfection in life. The many thoughts that travel through a Reed's mind may stimulate the Sun in surprising ways.

NINE CROCODILE

The domestic nature of Crocodile will be amplified with this placement. The Reed persona will empower this balanced day sign, with the number 9, to achieve great things. Aretha Franklin was able to express her connection to her primal feminine energy in a way that garnered her international recognition as a groundbreaking black, female entertainer. The Reed will help the Crocodile to think and express on a more elevated frequency. The Reed energy will also help the Crocodile come out of its lair and experience the world and not just the home.

TEN WIND

The supportive nature of this appointment within the Reed week will help the volatile Wind person maintain some stability. The rigid nature of the Reed day sign will be beneficial to the wayward Wind so that they can rise to positions of leadership. This Wind day sign will have a leaning toward philosophical and spiritual knowledge and communication. George Lucas, the creator of the Star Wars movies is a fine example of the ability of the Wind to focus and manifest in an impressive way with this placement.

ELEVEN NIGHT

The Reed's interest in high ideals and integrity can manifest in the Night day sign as having high principles. This is a challenging position for Night, and their achievements will come with a certain amount of controversy and struggle. They will be able to stand firm, with the help of the Reed, and accomplish greatness, no matter what the challenges. Abraham Lincoln was an 11 Night.

TWELVE SEED

The Seed person is caught in a mystery and surprise relationship with the Reed. This tends to make the Seed person motivated by the high standards of the Reed day sign. If they are able to roll with the punches, and find productive ways to express their uniqueness, they can achieve enormous success through dedication to their goals. The Seed may find themselves planted in many glorious, yet unexpected ways.

THIRTEEN SERPENT

This position within the Reed week empowers the Serpent. The high ideals and rigidity of the Reed will help the Serpent to use this power. This Serpent can be successful in leadership positions and use their charisma to the fullest.

The leadership potential of the Serpent day sign can be seen in the life of George W. Bush, the son of G.H. Bush, the 41st president of the United States. The call of leadership was strong within this family. Mr. Bush did make a lot of good reforms, but lost public support when the Serpent drive for power took over and he started the War on Terrorism. A 13 Serpent will always be in extreme situations that will somehow work out with the help of the steady Reed.

ONE TRANSFORMER
DEDICATION TO PROSPERITY AND COMMUNITY

The day sign of Transformer is really very concerned with the material world. They are good at creating abundance and have a strong motivation to help those around them to prosper. They are interested in the well being of their neighborhood and want to assist in creating peace, order and affluence for those in their lives. They are in touch with the spiritual energy of the earth and manifest this through practical applications such as aromatherapy, midwifery, shamanism and other forms of healing.

The day signs that are within the Transformer week are 2 Deer, 3 Star, 4 Offering, 5 Dog, 6 Monkey, 7 Road, 8 Reed, 9 Jaguar, 10 Eagle, 11 Wisdom, 12 Earth and 13 Flint.

TWO DEER

Even though this placement creates a mystery/surprise relationship with the Transformer, the effect upon the wandering Deer can be very beneficial. The Deer will be able to be more in tune with the energy of his community or core group. This position can bring the wealth that Transformer attracts to the Deer who uses their creativity and interest in artistic expression. The famous Country-Western music star Merle Haggard is a 2 Deer.

THREE STAR

These Star people will take on the interest in community that is important to the Transformer day sign. The Star proclivity toward debate can bring out a desire for political ambition. This is a challenge position for this Star, but that makes it all the more interesting to the Star person. Walter Mondale is a 3 Star person.

FOUR OFFERING

Emotional stability and focus upon others can be very positive for this day sign. The nature of Transformer week helps the Offering person to concentrate their powerful emotions in a productive way. That is because Offering is in a supportive relationship to the ruler of their week. This will help the Offering person glean benefit from their line of work and the people who they work with. This support can be seen in the career of famous 4 Offering person, the movie star Rock Hudson.

FIVE DOG

With the empowering interconnection between Dog and Transformer, this appointment will help Dog to take even greater involvement with their community and family. The often distracted Dog will have the motivation and determination necessary to be of consistent benefit to others. This placement will also help the Dog day sign to focus on creating prosperity in areas of real estate.

SIX MONKEY

Due to the correlation of surprise that the Transformer week puts upon the Monkey character, the 7 Monkey will take their predisposition toward being the volatile center of attention and have it work for them in unexpected ways. The Transformer influence will also give them an interest in social issues. The Monkey will bounce around in these arenas of life as the famous media personality Bill Moyers has done in his entertainment career.

SEVEN ROAD

The practical nature of Road can be enhanced by the Transformer ruler of the week, even though these two day signs are in opposition to each other. This challenging position can motivate the quiet Road person to manifest their interests in practical ways. The 7 Road people can often become financially abundant in working with real estate or home improvements. They may start a company to employ their community.

This position of Road and it's potential can be seen in the life of Robert Kennedy. He took the occupation of his family very seriously. His quiet personality and desire for sincere change was part of what attracted Americans to him. His passing was a loss to America and the world.

EIGHT REED

Within the Transformer week, the 8 Reed people will find support for their community and political drives.

The Transformer week will give the Reed the financial and community foundation to attain their political goals. This is apparent in the career of Sonny Bono. He decided to shake off the label of being Cher's counterpart and work in a more meaningful field of life: politics. He got the support of his small but prosperous community of Palm Springs, California where he focused his attention and energy.

NINE JAGUAR

The influence of Transformer can be very helpful to the 9 Jaguar in manifesting their dreams of material success. The Transformer influence for the Jaguar can translate into coming out to help and support their community. This can be seen in the life of the 9 Jaguar singer, Linda Ronstadt. She made a name for herself in the music world with her powerful voice. Then she decided to honor her Hispanic heritage and became devoted to the Latino community.

TEN EAGLE

The far ranging vision of the Eagle day sign was put to good use for one famous 10 Eagle, John Adams, the second president of the United States. The Transformer interest in politics was thrust upon Mr. Adams. He came to the aid of his country and used his Eagle foresight to help turn disenfranchised colonies into the United States of America.

ELEVEN WISDOM

The propensity of Wisdom to clean up messes left by others and rejuvenate the earth can be seen in the life of the 30th president of the United States, Calvin Coolidge. He came into office and cleaned up the scandal and corruption of his presidential predecessor. He regenerated the strength of the middle class and used the Transformer proclivity for prosperity to establish financial strength to the United States. His serious and practical Wisdom disposition brought healing and regeneration to America. Even though this is a challenging position for Wisdom, the unique combination of Transformer and Wisdom, and their love of the earth, can produce a positive life direction.

TWELVE EARTH

This is a supportive position within the Transformer week for this day sign. It can help bring stability to the extremely active mind of the Earth day sign. With the support and direction that the Transformer day sign provides, this person will be able to direct their mental energies to be of service to themselves and their community. They will be able to put their ideas into action and manifest their potentials in business or other careers.

THIRTEEN FLINT

With this station within the Transformer week, this Flint day sign is empowered to achieve great success in what they feel is important. They may decide to use their natural healing ability for the good of their community. The Flint person may also feel a desire to work in legal areas to help those who are downtrodden or who have been victims of injustice.

ONE STORM
CHEERFUL AND COMPASSIONATE HELPER

The child-like simplicity and caring of the Storm personality brings much needed feelings of compassion and nurturing to the world. Their desire to be of service and their connection to the sub conscious make them great friends, partners and guides in the creative process.

The day signs that are influenced by the Storm personality are 2 Sun, 3 Crocodile, 4 Wind, 5 Night, 6 Seed, 7 Serpent, 8 Transformer, 9 Deer, 10 Star, 11 Offering, 12 Dog and 13 Monkey.

TWO SUN

This can be a great influence upon the detached and often aloof Sun. The supportive connection of the West and the South will make these Suns more compassionate and caring for others. This stimulus can help Sun have a better relationship with all the people in their lives. These Suns can do well in the teaching and healing professions.

The life of author Hermann Hesse is an example of a Sun that had a spiritual and compassionate focus. His book Siddhartha illustrated the life of Buddha. The book illustrates the Sun's royal roots that become transformed with the compassion and empathy of Storm.

THREE CROCODILE

This challenging position for the Crocodile can actually push the Crocodile out of their complacent primal lair and motivate them on a creative level. The stimulation of the Storm energy to be compassionate and share with many can arouse the Crocodile to work in fields where they are using their basic nurturing instincts to help those they do not know. The love of family will be enhanced with this focus.

FOUR WIND

The wind person may be in for some surprises with this placement in the Storm week. The Wind person may be in touch with their sub conscious and have the desire to experience creativity in many different ways. With the unexpected stimulus that this position provides, the Wind person may have many powerful spiritual experiences.

The Pop icon Michael Jackson was a 4 Wind person that not only was in touch with the gateway to creativity that Storm opens, but was a chameleon who changed his work and appearance as often as the wind changes.

FIVE NIGHT

Due to the empowering stimulus of Storm upon this day sign that is also ruled by the West, the Night person's love of family will be amplified. Creating security for their family will be very strong within the Night person. The Storm influence will also help the usually serious and contemplative Night person to be more expressive. They will have more compassion for others and be willing to help others complete their goals. The Storm energy will also stimulate the latent intuitive and energetic healing abilities of the Night person.

SIX SEED

The positive connection between Storm and Seed will help the Seed person to tune into their creative skills. The sensual, sexual Seed disposition will be infused with compassion and caring for those people that are in this Seed's life. This placement might just make a family person out of this Seed. This connection to the sub conscious will also arouse the intuitive abilities of the Seed temperament.

F. Scott Fitzgerald is a classic example of the Seed's challenges in this placement. Even though his love for Zelda was representative of the Strom dedication to loved ones, the Seed personality wanted to express itself. The Seed's tendency to overdue was evident in Fitzgerald's excessive life style that caused him much trauma during his life.

SEVEN SERPENT

Even though this placement within the Storm week can be challenging for the Serpent, Storm seems to bring out the best in all the day signs that it touches. The Storm persuasion will bring out the intellectual abilities of the Serpent. It will elevate the primordial Serpent power to help others and be compassionate instead of using their hypnotic influence to rule over others. These

Serpents can become teachers, psychologists and healers that truly care for others.

EIGHT TRANSFORMER

The relationship of mystery and surprise for the Transformer person, born in the Storm week, may coerce the grounded and materially focused Transformer to call on their intuitive and healing abilities. This appointment to the Storm week will probably force the Transformer person to develop this connection through circumstances that are out of their control. Once Transformer has accepted the opening of these aspects of their persona, they will find that they may be called on to make many sacrifices for others as well. The rewards of helping others will come to this Transformer person, but in arenas of life that they did not expect.

The Microsoft mogul Bill Gates is an example of a Transformer's ability to manifest abundance. The surprise factor for Mr. Gates is the incredible financial abundance and ability to help others that he has manifested.

NINE DEER

The wandering nature of the Deer may be redirected so that they are more attached and concerned about others. Due to the empowering influence of the Storm day sign, the Deer will be able to bring out their love of art and creativity through personal expression, instead of only experiencing art. With the Storm's help, the Deer temperament will find it easier to settle down and commit to others.

TEN STAR

The mental complexity and love of details that is within the Star disposition will get a supportive boost from this placement. The compassion and caring of the Storm day sign will help the Star person to use their love of intellectual stimulation in a positive way. Storm will help the Star to get in touch with their innovative ability and use it to help others. Storm helps Star get outside of themselves and become successful.

The creative ability that comes from Storm can be seen in the career of 10 Star Jack Nicholson, the actor. Mr. Nicholson has taken his love of being in front of the public and has had a very creative career, playing a wide variety of intellectually stimulating, diverse roles.

ELEVEN OFFERING

The Offering person will find that the challenge of the Storm restlessness will cause this already high strung day sign to be even more emotional. This will create a situation where the Offering person will have to address this aspect of their nature and find productive, life enhancing ways to express this energy. The Storm day sign's desire to be of service may bring out the true essence of leadership within the Offering person.

TWELVE DOG

The restlessness that is innate within the Dog temperament will be stimulated by the Storm day sign.

This can create problems for the Dog person. Due to the mystery/surprise connection between Dog and Storm, there may by some unexpected reactions for the Dog person in the areas of family and relationship. On the other hand, the loving nature of the Dog will be enhanced by the concern for others that the Storm day sign carries. The Dog day sign will be motivated to use more of their mental ability and may become an educator or express themselves in some form of art.

THIRTEEN MONKEY

This position for Monkey will amplify their active, artistic, innovative talents. This is an empowering position for the Monkey. With this placement, the Monkey will not be as self centered. The Monkey day sign will not feel the overpowering need to be in the spotlight of attention all the time. This position in the Storm week will help the Monkey person be more compassionate, thoughtful and helpful to those around them. Storm will bring out the ability of the Monkey to think of others first.

Barbara Streisand is a classic Monkey who loves to perform and has had a great variety of roles. The power of 13 can be seen in her ability to rise to a position of superstardom with the help of the creative Storm day sign.

ONE ROAD
MANIFESTATION OF GRACE AND HUMILITY

Even though the Road personality is usually quiet and easy going, they can shine forth in many practicable areas of life. They have success in fields where they can find peace and security and help others.

The day signs found within the Road week are 2 Reed, 3 Jaguar, 4 Eagle, 5 Wisdom, 6 Earth, 7 Flint, 8 Storm, 9 Sun, 10 Crocodile, 11 Wind, 12 Night and 13 Seed.

TWO REED

The rather intellectual and lofty Reed will find that there will be many unexpected opportunities to work on their appreciation of the simplicity of life. These awareness and situations may come to the Reed person without seeking them out. The Reed person will be more relaxed and find that the simple things in life can be rewarding. This appointment will also bring out the desire of the Reed to have a loving relationship and be more accepting of their partner's faults.

THREE JAGUAR

The Jaguars born into this position in the Road week will find that they will go through many challenges to heal the anger that that may erupt from time to time. Both Jaguar and Road have dispositions that suppress many of their feelings and needs. The Road stimulus will challenge the Jaguar to be in relationships that will cause them to be more concerned about the well being of their partner. As the Jaguar learns to work with this influence, they will become more connected to the people in their lives and think of them first. The commitment to relationship will bring out the best in the Jaguar person.

FOUR EAGLE

The soaring disposition of the Eagle, with it's desire to be independent will be humbled by the simplicity and down to earth nature of the Road day sign. This is a supportive placement for the Eagle, so the lessons that the easy going Road day sign have to teach Eagle will be painless for the most part. The Eagle will enjoy having a lot of people around and socializing. The Eagle person will be able to expand their perspective on life.

John F Kennedy, president of the United States, was able to see the elevated perspective of life that is natural to the Eagle, yet presented the gracious persona of Road. Mr. Kennedy was dedicated to helping the common man, which is part of the Road make-up.

FIVE WISDOM

Due to this empowering placement, the serious and success oriented temperament of Wisdom is softened by the kindness and casual manner of the Road day sign. The Road day sign will bring out the desire for a loving relationship within the Wisdom person.

The importance of relationship can be seen in the life of entertainer George Burns. He became famous for portraying the serious straight man so that his beloved comedian wife Gracie Allen could shine.

SIX EARTH

The rapid fire mind of the Earth person will get surprises in life that will propel them to use their minds in practical, if unusual ways. The Earth person may fall unexpectedly into success with the help of the consistent and methodical influence of the Road day sign.

Alfred Hitchcock, the film maker of thrillers such as The Birds, pioneered the way for horror films in the 21st century. Even though he had innovative ideas that are commonplace for Earth people, he presented the soft spoken, casual manner of the Road day sign. His Road personality made him as famous as his movies.

SEVEN FLINT

The dedication to a cause that is within the disposition of the Flint person can be brought out in this appointment in the Road week. The natural tendency to persevere for a reason that the Flint person feels is worthwhile can challenge this day sign to bring out the best in themselves.

Dorothy Hamill, the Olympic ice skating champion, was able to combine the Flint dedication and adherence to a goal with the Road qualities of sacrifice, ambition and the ability to do repetitive activities. These opposing day signs worked together to manifest beauty and achievement.

EIGHT STORM

The supportive combination of these two day signs can bring about a very loving and imaginative person. The support that the Storm person receives from the Road day sign will amplify their focus toward friends and family. Both these day signs have a strong leaning toward relationship. The Storm person will not only find joy with the Road influence in relationships but will also have the emotional expression and playfulness that may be lacking from the Road nature. This combination can bring a happy home for the sensitive, intuitive Storm person.

NINE SUN

The Sun that falls into the Road week will find that the empowering relationship they have will help to heal the great tragedy that often befalls a Sun person: the inability to have lasting relationships. The giving and strength of the humble Road day sign will work upon the proud Sun to help this kingly day sign appreciate the small, simple beauties of life. This position within the Road week will enable the Sun to know the joy that lasting relationships can bring to life.

TEN CROCODILE

The impact of the mystery and surprise that constitutes the relationship between Crocodile and Road may lead the Crocodile person to some unexpected turns in life. Both Crocodile and Road are home bodies and love family. Yet the ambition that Road can display can work against the primal nature of the Crocodile.

This dilemma can be seen in the rock star Janice Joplin. She followed the desire of Road to be successful, but did not have the stable family that a Crocodile needs. Unfortunately Janis was not able to handle the success that the Road influence brought into her life. She got caught up in the only family that was around her: other rock stars that were addicted to harmful drugs. When this Crocodile is motivated by success, they need to have a quiet, stable family in their home.

ELEVEN WIND

Even though this combination is a challenging one, it worked very well for the Televangelist Billy Graham. He was able to use his communication skills to reach millions of people with his message.

One can see the Road impact upon this Wind person. The temperament of Road is stable and focused on home and family values. The Road influence was able to give this Wind person the stability to be successful in his mission to bring his ideals about god and family to the world.

TWELVE NIGHT

Both Road and Night have a desire for security and success. This supportive combination can be seen in the life of the Greek shipping tycoon Aristole Onassis. He liked the quiet life that appeals to the Night person. Yet Night is very security conscious. This combination was able to give him the ability to persevere in business and still have a quiet yet opulent life style.

THIRTEEN SEED

Seed and Road are a powerful combination. This is a very positive placement for the Seed person. They can use their desire for achievement and also have the nurturing of family life. The indulgent Seed will find that they are more interested in the relationship aspects of sexuality then just the experience. With this combination, the Seed person will have the stamina and focus to be successful in business and family.

ONE SERPENT
CHARISMA AND PASSION

Serpent energy is very dynamic and even hypnotic. The Serpent energy is valuable when focused toward larger than life performances be they in the home, stage or office. Those born in this week will feel the sexual and transformative energy of the Serpent within their personality.

Those day signs impacted by Serpent energy are 2 Transformer, 3 Deer, 4 Star, 5 Offering, 6 Dog, 7 Monkey, 8 Road, 9 Reed, 10 Jaguar, 11Eagle, 12 Wisdom and 13 Earth.

TWO TRANSFORMER

This placement within the Serpent week may cause the Transformer person to be very religious or focus on spiritual aspects of life. The Transformer day sign is usually very down-to-earth, so the Serpent energy will bring out the spiritual inclination within the Transformer person. The Serpent stimulus can also cause these people to be very dramatic and emotional. The famous dare devil Evel Knievel is a good example of how the influence of the day sign of the week one is born in can overshadow the day sign of birth. He has become all that the Serpent energy can bring out in a person: charisma and reckless intensity. Being a Transformer, he used his passion to make money as well.

THREE DEER

The Serpent persuasion can turn the easy going Deer into a passionate and sexual being. This Deer person will have very strong opinions that will be hard for them to release. The challenging relationship between Deer and Serpent can cause many difficulties that the Deer person will have to overcome.

Meryl Streep is a 3 Deer person who has been able to turn the Serpent's drive for creativity into an incredible, diverse career. The charisma of Serpent and the Deer's love of art and beauty have helped her to manifest a position of prominence in the motion picture industry.

FOUR STAR

This can really be a very interesting placement for the Star person. It can amplify their ability to go before the public and captivate them. This is the case with Bette Midler. Thanks to the Serpent energy, the magic of her voice brought her a lot of fame that is not usually part of the Star character. It is interesting that she is not known for being addicted to drugs, which can be a Star problem, but she became famous for portraying a drug-addicted singer in The Rose.

FIVE OFFERING

The empowering effect of Serpent upon the Offering person can cause them to have very strong emotions and take dynamic action. The natural inclination of the Offering person to be an entertainer can be amplified by this combination. This can translate into a career in entertainment, religion or politics. The Offering person can use their double shot of charisma to their advantage in any area where leadership is needed.

A 5 Offering person that let his passions and emotions get the best of him is former president Bill Clinton. Even though this is an empowering placement, as an Offering person, Bill got out of control with the influence of Serpent's potent sexuality.

SIX DOG

The Serpent will bring out the leadership qualities in this placement of the Dog day sign. It will also amplify the basic tendency of the Dog person to be interested in sex. This is a supportive position for the Dog day sign, but even so, too much of a good thing can create problems for the easy going Dog. The Serpent day sign will also bring out the desire for leadership in the Dog. The Dog day sign does not usually like to be in leadership positions, but with the help of the Serpent, the Dog can be an impassioned and successful leader.

SEVEN MONKEY

Due to the challenging relationship of Serpent and Monkey energy, the Monkey person, who naturally likes to be center stage, will have an even stronger desire to be in the center of all that is happening. Unfortunately, this will probably cause the Monkey person to learn some unpleasant lessons before they are able to find balance in this area of life. Serpent's natural sex appeal could also cause problems for the gregarious Monkey.

EIGHT ROAD

The humble Road person will probably find that they end up in some surprising situations due to the sexual energy and emotional intensity that comes along with the Serpent influence. The hidden emotions and the tendency to get their feelings hurt will be amplified and the Road person may find themselves expressing a variety of emotions unexpectedly. The Serpent may also bring out the desire of the Road person to seek positions of power.

NINE REED

The empowering combination of Reed and Serpent can bring out the ardor in the usually reserved and idealistic Reed. This residency in the Serpent week will bring out the emotional side of the Reed and give them more intensity. There will also be a fair share of allure for the Reed day sign. This can be seen in the life of the dynamic singer, 9 Reed Judy Garland. She was known not only for her fantastic voice but also for her fervent performances that many will never forget.

TEN JAGUAR

With this placement within the Serpent week, the Jaguar will find that they are comfortable coming out of their cave and getting into the spotlight. For those

Jaguars that are interested in spirituality, the supportive nature of the relationship of Serpent and Jaguar will bring about very strong mystical experiences, visions and connections to the sub conscious. The Jaguar person may be interested in psychology and other forms of emotional healing. With the power that this combination manifests within the Jaguar person, it is important for them to honor the proper use of the forces that can come forth from within them and not take advantage of the influence over others.

ELEVEN EAGLE

The position of the Eagle within the Serpent week will bring about many potent experiences for the Eagle. Even though this is a challenging assignment for the Eagle, it will cause them to use their expanded vision to be of help to humanity. The Serpent will give the Eagle person a warm, motivated personality that will help them be more connected to people then the usually aloof Eagle.

Eleven Eagle Phil Donahue, the talk show host, seemed to feel that it was his mission to give his audiences a broad view of humanity. Mr. Donahue's program was loved and appreciated by millions of people. The Serpent gave him the caring personality that is necessary to win over his viewers. The challenge element between Eagle and Serpent can be seen in the usually controversial topics that were the basis of Mr. Donahue's programs.

TWELVE WISDOM

The somber Wisdom is definitely in for some surprises by landing within the Serpent week. The Serpent will help Wisdom to have more personality and excitement in their lives. The Serpent will also help the Wisdom to intensify the Wisdom's desires for success and achievement. The already driven Wisdom will be able to harness their storehouse of energy to realize their goals. This tireless devotion to their goals will take Wisdom farther along the path of accomplishment then Wisdom would ever have expected.

THIRTEEN EARTH

The mentally eruptive personality of the Earth person will be amplified by the empowering connection to the Serpent. Earth already is filled with many ideas and thoughts and the Serpent influence can bring out the brilliance and genius of the Earth person.

The potent stimulus of the Serpent upon the Earth person is well illustrated in the life of the inventor and statesman Benjamin Franklin. This 13 Earth person was literally bubbling over with ideas that he turned into inventions. His interests were very diverse for his time. His help was invaluable in forming the United States of America at a delicate time in our country's history. The Serpent gave him a healthy sexual nature that made him infamous as well as famous during his life.

ONE FLINT
THE HEALER AND THE CRUSADER

Those born into the Flint week will have an inclination for learning, communication and fighting for a cause. They will also be interested in healing and helping people improve their lives.

The day signs that fall within the Flint week are 2 Storm, 3 Sun, 4 Crocodile, 5 Wind, 6 Night, 7 Seed, 8 Serpent, 9 Transformer, 10 Deer, 11 Star, 12 Offering and 13 Dog.

TWO STORM

Those born into this day sign will have the benefit of the communication abilities that Storm may not always possess. The loving heart and desire for relationships and family will be intermingled with the Flint desire to communicate.

A famous actor, 2 Storm Henry Fonda, exemplifies a beautiful blend of these qualities. He had the soft spoken and gentle manner of the Storm. He was in the motion picture industry, which is Flint communication on a world wide scale. His love of his family, which is a powerful Storm trait, can be seen in the fact that he brought his family, his daughter Jane and his son Peter into the motion picture business.

THREE SUN

This position of challenge within the Flint week can give a great calling to be of service to the Sun person.

The innate desire to carry on traditions within the Sun persona can be stimulated by the Flint's desire to bring these truths to light.

In the area of relationships, Flint will only compound the difficulties that the Sun person has with relationships. Both of these day signs are very idealistic about relationships. It will take some work for the Sun day sign to overcome the challenge of this position to find and maintain a relationship that works for them.

FOUR CROCODILE

This placement of the slow going Crocodile with the perfectionist Flint can be seen in the life of the movie star Joan Crawford. Even though she was a 4 Crocodile, she was strongly influenced by the Flint ruler of her birth week. Communications was her main area of life. She dedicated a great deal to that field. Her day sign Crocodile motivated her to adopt children and have her own family. As revealed by her children, she combined the Crocodile desire for family, domination and control with the perfectionist nature of the Flint.

FIVE WIND

This is an empowering position for the Wind person. This placement will give the Wind person a strong leaning toward using their mind and mechanical abilities such as an engineer or draftsman. This station within the Flint week will help this person to stick to projects and maintain a focus that can often elude the Wind personality.

The 5 Wind person will probably have the relationship problems of Flint and Wind combined. The fickle nature of Wind together with the enabling nature of Flint can lead to many complications in marriage and business.

SIX NIGHT

Due to the mystery/surprise relationship between Night and Flint, this placement of Night may find some surprises in achieving the security that the Night person so strongly desires. There may be unexpected twists and turns in the plans that the Night person wishes to carry out.

The good news in all of this is that Flint will help Night to hold fast in the face of challenges. Even though the Night person may have a few monkey wrenches thrown into their plans they will also be helped by Flint to keep going and follow through until the goal is reached.

SEVEN SEED

Even though this is a challenging position for the Seed person, the high ideals and dedication to achieve a goal that is part of the Flint make up will be helpful to the Seed person. Flint also helps the Seed person to find their unique slice of life and stand up for their individuality.

This can be seen the life of the 7 Seed Paul Gauguin. He sought a lifestyle that was in harmony with his temperament and desire for sexual expression. After many unsuccessful attempts, he finally found peace in the

South Seas. Most of his art reflects the unique life he was finally able to create.

EIGHT SERPENT

Due to the supportive relationship between Flint and Serpent, it will be fairly easy for the Serpent person to find an environment and course of action that will be in harmony with their nature. The Flint tendency to sacrifice for others will help the Serpent to find compromise in relationships. They will not have to be the center of attention and the leader, which is usually the way with Serpent personalities. The Serpent person will be able to find that they can work in harmony with others and be successful in their life goals.

NINE TRANSFORMER

The position of Transformer in the Flint week can be a very commanding placement for the Transformer day sign. The empowering energy between Flint and Transformer will help the Transformer person to be very successful at all they undertake. The Transformer day sign is already interested in helping others. With the help of Flint, The Transformer person will be victorious in achieving their goals for themselves and their community. Flint gives Transformer more devotion to others and more impetus to be of service.

TEN DEER

This appointment to the Flint week can bring unexpected obstacles for the Deer person to overcome. The focus of intention to complete goals that is part of the Flint make up will be helpful to the Deer person in completing projects and remaining focused on their desired result.

Barbara Walters has used her 10 Deer and Flint potentials effectively. She has been able to honor the Deer's need to be free to roam the world with her work. The Flint has helped her to maintain her focus and become a celebrity in the field of communication.

ELEVEN STAR

Even though this is a challenging position for a Star to land in, the single-mindedness of the Flint week will help the Star person, who can sometimes be wayward and overindulgent, stay on track. With the help of Flint, the Star person will be able to pay attention to the other people in their lives. Since the Flint has the warrior energy within it, the Star person may be called on to maintain a serious perspective on life. The sacrificing way of the Flint will help the Star person to have a life that has space for others to flourish.

TWELVE OFFERING

The passionate thoughts and feelings of the Offering person will find a harmonious outlet in their lives with the support of the Flint day sign. This placement will help Offering find focus for their inclinations. The Flint will help the Offering person dedicate themselves to the goals that they feel so strongly that they want to achieve. The high number of this placement is assisted by Flint to be successful in leadership positions.

THIRTEEN DOG

With this position in the Flint week, the mental abilities of the dog will be stimulated and elevated. The empowering connection between these two day signs will assist the Dog in using their communication skills and intellectual prowess to be of greater assistance to whoever they consider their "pack" to be. The Flint day sign will also assist the Dog to live up to the ideals of loyalty that the Dog feels for family and friends. With the help of Flint, the Dog can rise to leadership positions and find success in helping those to whom they are dedicated.

ONE MONKEY
PERFORMANCE AND POLITICS

The high energy and creativity of the Monkey brings playfulness and creativity to the day signs in its week. The artistic flair of this day sign along with the desire to be the center of attention will be infused into the lives of those in the Monkey week.

The day signs that are within this week are 2 Road, 3 Reed, 4 Jaguar, 5 Eagle, 6 Wisdom, 7 Earth, 8 Flint, 9 Storm, 10 Sun, 11 Crocodile, 12 Wind and 13 Night.

TWO ROAD

With the support of the Monkey day sign, the Road person will more than likely want to let go of the humble nature of Road and come out on stage. If not center stage, then the Road person will definitely feel the desire to be involved in the stage. The Road person may even want to turn their money making abilities toward projects or work that are creative and entertaining.

This Road person will probably not have the usual timid, soft spoken nature of the usual Road person. These people make HREE REEDentertain in their homes and enjoy parties.

THREE REED

The Monkey flair for public presentation will help this Reed person to take their ideas and philosophies to the world. The natural inclination of the Reed to uphold ideals will enable this Reed person to be more outward going and share their political and philosophical concepts on a broader, public scale.

This is illustrated in the life of 3 Reed Annie Besant. She started out as a political organizer and then turned her attention to the spiritual teachings of the Far East. She helped found the Theosophical Society in the early 1900s. She used her flair for politics to head several organizations to assist causes in India.

FOUR JAGUAR

This Jaguar finds them in a week that brings surprises. The nature of the Monkey is to be public and the Jaguar likes to be soft spoken and hide. The Jaguar person may be attracted to events that are produced for the public, even though they won't want to be in the limelight themselves. As long as the Jaguar person does not take themselves too seriously, they will have fun and be entertained in life.

FIVE EAGLE

The Monkey seems to bring the lighter side of life to all those born within it's week. This is the effect that the Monkey has on the high flying Eagle. This position in the Monkey week is empowering to the Eagle and at the same time, brings the lofty, detached Eagle down to earth for some simple pleasures in life. The influence of Monkey can stimulate the Eagle toward the entertainment field, as well as teaching. With the Monkey's tendency to bounce around a lot, the Eagle may have problems having a committed relationship.

5 Eagle Gertrude Stein, the renowned art collector, was able to soar to the heights of the Eagle's vision. She established art galleries and collected the works of the great artists of her time such as Renoir, Cezanne, Matisse and Picasso.

SIX WISDOM

The lucky Wisdom that lands in this week will also find a bit of relief from the serious side of the Wisdom nature. The Monkey helps Wisdom stimulate their ability for entertainment and politics.

The supportive energy between Wisdom and Monkey can be seen in the life of 6 Wisdom comedian Carol Burnett. Wisdom is not a day sign that would naturally be drawn to entertainment. The Monkey qualities that often came out in many of Ms. Burnett's characters, created a dynamite combination of abilities that gave Ms. Burnett the reputation of being a versatile performer and the Wisdom focus to maintain a prominent, busy career.

SEVEN EARTH

With their desire to be a part of innovative experiences, the Earth person will be motivated to take up the new and even unproven. The challenging relationship between Monkey and Earth will push these people to take action on their forward thinking ideas and even be out in front of the public.

This is the case with 7 Earth astronaut Frank Borman, who was the commander of the Apollo 8, the first spacecraft to fly around the moon. During his life, Mr. Borman was also the CEO of Eastern airlines.

EIGHT FLINT

The mystery and surprise relationship of Flint and Monkey will probably bring the serious Flint person out into the spotlight. This may be unexpected, but it will stimulate the Flint person to be in the public and focused upon their careers.

The playfulness of the Monkey can be seen in the career of 8 Flint Art Linkletter. This light hearted radio and television personality exhibited more of the Monkey persona then that of the nose-to-the grindstone Flint. Mr. Linkletter is known for the joy he found in the everyday comedic relief of children and other mundane areas of life. Even though he was born a Flint, it is easy to see how the Monkey energy dominated and enriched his life.

NINE STORM

The emotional youthfulness of the Storm day sign is enhanced with this empowering placement within the Monkey week. The creative expression of the Storm is boosted by the playfulness of the Monkey. This creates a lively combination for performing and any type of creative art.

The Storm predisposition for imitation is amplified with the Monkey appointment. This makes Storm people excellent teachers who are happy teaching what others have discovered.

TEN SUN

With the support of the Monkey energy for this day sign, it is possible for the kingly nature of the Sun to be powerfully realized. This positive placement will help the Sun person to be charismatic and use the position of public authority with grace and ease.

The positive, supportive combination of Monkey and Sun can be seen in the life of 10 Sun Pope John Paul II. With Sun as his basic nature and the Monkey as his friend and supporter, this man became one of the most popular popes in history. The Monkey energy within him gave him the interest in getting off the papal throne and going out into the world. The cleverness of the Monkey mind gave him the ability to learn 14 languages and brought the image of a loving head of the Catholic Church to the planet.

ELEVEN CROCODILE

The challenging interaction between the Monkey and the Crocodile can catapult the Crocodile out of it's hideaway and into the spotlight. This placement can cause the home loving Crocodile to work hard to express the creativity that they feel inside themselves.

The need for creative expression can be seen in the life of 11 Crocodile Joan Baez. This political activist and songstress had to face a lot of challenges to get her message and feelings known during the Vietnam War. She has strongly felt the Monkey interest in politics and fought for many special interest political groups over the years. This is just one of many examples of how the week a person is born into can influence them more then the day sign of their birth.

TWELVE WIND

The position of the Wind within the Monkey week can lead this volatile day sign into some interesting and unexpected situations. The Wind day sign likes to travel around so the Monkey propensity for movement and attention will bring the Wind person into some unanticipated experiences. The combination of Monkey and Wind do make for some great communication experiences. Those Wind people born into this assignment will be able to use their talents for music and dance as well as writing to create some beautiful and entertaining projects. These people may go into teaching as well.

THIRTEEN NIGHT

Even though the Monkey will probably drag the serious Night person out of their comfort zone, this empowering residency within the Monkey week can help the shy, earnest yet creative Night make the most of their talents.

This is evidenced in the life of 13 Night Roy Rogers, the singing cowboy. Roy was able to stay within his comfort zone, cowboy life, and become a radio and television star. He created the financial security that Night people need while using his Monkey-inspired creative talents of singing and acting. Roy expressed the Monkey desire to use their hands when he did twirling tricks with his lasso!

ONE SEED
INDIVIDUALITY AND SEXUALITY

The Seed is another day sign that is very creative. The essence of the Seed energy revolves around their personal creative expression or uniqueness of who they sense they are. With the metaphor of the tree being contained within the seed, Seed people have great energy, sexuality and artistic expression within them that needs to be expressed. Due to their dynamic energy, the Seed person also makes for a good leader or role model if they are able to focus their force in a positive way.

The day signs that fall within the Seed week are 2 Serpent, 3 Transformer, 4 Deer, 5 Star, 6 Offering, 7 Dog, 8 Monkey, 9 Road, 10 Reed, 11 Jaguar, 12 Eagle and 13 Wisdom.

TWO SERPENT

This relationship of mystery and surprise can be very powerful for the Serpent born into the Seed week. Both these day signs have the focus of sexuality and personal expression. The famous 2 Serpent, Mae West, found a perfect use for her vibrant sexuality and personal goals. If you have seen any of her old movies, you will know that she glides through her movies like the Serpent that she was.

THREE TRANSFORMER

This is a very good position for the Transformer day sign. Even though Transformer is in a challenging relationship with the Seed day sign, this can push the Transformer person to go beyond their quiet nature and to really express their individuality and creativity.

It is easy to see these qualities in the famous 3 Transformer, Paul McCartney of the Beatles. He was able to express himself through his music that was controversial at the time. The Transformer energy helped him to stay on track with his music and is now the richest songwriter in the world.

FOUR DEER

The tendency toward the eccentric can be seen in the life of the famous 4 Deer, Prince Charles of Great Britain. His inclination to roam can be seen by his world travels and his desire to help the unfortunate. His eccentric love life became the focus of the media for years as he carried on an affair while married to Princess Diana. The Seed need for sexual expression, no matter the cost, has weighed heavily upon his life. In this case, the supportive nature of Seed and Deer's need for freedom in relationships created inner drives that he could not escape.

FIVE STAR

Through this empowering placement within the Seed week, the renowned 5 Star, Billy Jean King, was able to rise to a position of world prominence in the tennis world. Then her empire came crumbling down when she honored her Seed desire for distinctive sexual expression. She paid a great price, both financially and professionally for declaring her sexual inclinations. She has gone on to make strong holds for women within the sports field.

SIX OFFERING

The creative ability of those ruled by the direction of the East can benefit from the stability and goals of prosperity that the Seed day sign can bring. Even though this is a mystery/surprise relationship between Seed and Offering, the uncompromising drive of the Offering person mixed with the Seed's desire for prominence and expression can be seen in the life of 6 Offering television news caster, Walter Cronkite. He started his career at the beginning of the television era and rose to fame doing what he loved to do: report what is happening in the world.

Another famous 6 Offering person, mob boss Al Capone, took a less positive direction and found fame in his work as well. The moral of this story is: the mystery/surprise connection between Offering and Seed can go in many directions.

SEVEN DOG

Through the challenging connection between Seed and Dog, the simple Dog person may be stimulated to bring about their potential. The loyalty of the Dog personality and the willingness to fight for their community can be seen in the life of the notorious fighter for his people, the head of the Palestine Liberation Organization, 7 Dog Yasser Arafat. His extreme sense of loyalty to his people and his willingness to achieve his goals through any means shows how powerful this combination can be.

EIGHT MONKEY

This placement within the Seed week can have a very beneficial effect upon the bouncy Monkey personality. The supportive position within the Seed week can help the Monkey person to become prosperous with their talents. The Seed can help the Monkey to find a productive outlet for their creative energy and help them to focus their attention to manifest what they are capable of doing. The Seed's ability for leadership can bring the Monkey into the spotlight and help them to be successful.

NINE ROAD

This appointment to the Seed week can be a very advantageous spot for the humble and easy going Road person. The Seed's drive for success and recognition can be seen in the life of television host of the news show 20/20 and the Today Show, 9 Road Hugh Downs. Even with all the prestige the years for his accomplishments, he still presents the soft spoken, gracious persona of the Road personality.

TEN REED

With the help of the Seed persona, this position for the Reed can bring out unexpected abilities and careers. The Seed potential to obsess over sex can be seen in the life of the famous 10 Reed, Sigmund Freud. Mr. Freud was a pioneer in the field of psychoanalysis. Even though his ideas were of the highest motivation, that defines the Reed nature, the mystery/surprise connection has made Mr. Freud famous for his emphasis on sexual drives. That is definitely a Seed area of focus. You can see the distinctive viewpoint of the Seed nature peeking through in Mr. Freud's reputation. Over a hundred years later his name brings to mind his unique sexual perspectives.

ELEVEN JAGUAR

Even though this is a challenging position for the Jaguar, it creates a person that is able to go against the grain of whatever is happening in their lives and find success. This ability, of meeting and surmounting a challenge can be seen in the life of controversial baby doctor, 11 Jaguar Benjamin Spock. His book on babies and child care revolutionized ideas about child rearing. He was also an anti Viet Nam war supporter and received much criticism for that view. Challenge and controversy was a big part of this ground breaking person's life.

TWELVE EAGLE

This supportive placement within the Seed week helped legendary film star, 12 Eagle Humphrey Bogart, achieve prominence. This Eagle received great support from his placement within the Seed week. He had the vision to see into the future of entertainment when he switched from stage to motion pictures after the great depression. He soared to the top of his profession and led the way for a new cinema hero to emerge. His unique style of acting was helped by the Seed to enable his individuality stand out.

THIRTEEN WISDOM

With the empowering connection between Seed and Wisdom, the usually quiet and serious Wisdom can find the means to achieve their goals of prosperity. Both Seed and Wisdom are focused on achieving financial abundance. With the Seed influence, the Wisdom person will probably be more independent and expressive. The Wisdom person may be very popular and also be able to set an example for those they love and their community. The Wisdom person may even be moved to take on leadership positions, which is due to the empowering influence of the Seed day sign.

ONE EARTH
ERUPTIONS OF LOGIC AND IMAGINATION

This day sign was given this name by the Aztecs and later the Mayas because this day sign is constantly erupting, like a volcano, with ideas. It's original name is earthquake. Earth people come up with brilliant ideas and solutions to problems. Their greatest asset is their ability to find practical applications to their ideas.

The day signs within the Earth week are 2 Flint, 3 Storm, 4 Sun, 5 Crocodile, 6 Wind, 7 Night, 8 Seed, 9 Serpent, 10 Transformer, 11 Deer, 12 Rabbit and 13 Offering.

TWO FLINT

The mental ability of this Flint person is amplified, due to the supportive nature of this connection between Earth and Flint. This placement within the Earth week gives the Flint person a very quick mind and practical applications on how to use their ideas. This person can be very quick witted, yet soft spoken. They will also have very good mechanical dexterity and be good at solving mechanical problems.

THREE STORM

The Storm person that finds themselves within the Earth week will find that they may have to go through struggles and challenges to express their ingenuity. The connection to the sub conscious and creativity is very strong within the Storm person. The challenge to the

180

Storm person will be to not let obstacles hinder their vision.

This can be seen in the life of the legendary entertainer, 3 Storm, Gypsy Rose Lee. She was propelled into burlesque where she expressed her creativity that is part the Strom nature, and became known for her wit and style. She also went on to use her Earth inspired mind to write books and films for the movie industry.

FOUR SUN

This can be a challenging position for the Sun day sign, even though this is a placement that brings mystery and surprise. This can convey unexpected difficulties in the areas of relationship and personal life. The difficulty that Sun has with relationship can be amplified with this position in the Earth week. On the bright side, the imagination and ingenuity of the Earth can also be enhanced for the Sun individual in many artistic ways.

FIVE CROCODILE

With the support of the Earth week, this Crocodile can achieve many great accomplishments in their lives. The influence of the Earth can bring the Crocodile out of the primal marshes of their home and family and into the realms of invention and originality.

The powerful stimulus of the Earth upon the Crocodile person is evidenced in the life of 5 Crocodile Thomas Edison. The Wizard of Menlo Park appears to be a classic example of an Earth person, with his many ideas that manifested into inventions that changed the world.

Mr. Edison did have a strong Crocodile streak within him. He married twice and had six children.

SIX WIND

With the support of the Earth day sign, this residency of Wind can bring about great accomplishments. This placement may create a bit of instability however. Both Earth and Wind can be erratic mentally and emotionally. The Wind person needs a lot of time to be quiet and connect with their own inner sense of stability in order to function successfully in the world.

These two day signs combined in an interesting way in the life of 6 Wind Frank L Baum, an author best known for his children's masterpiece, the Wizard of Oz. The communication aspect of Mr. Baum's life was amplified with the help of the Earth day sign. Found within his writing, that manifested a century later, are the progressive Earth ideas for the television, lap top computer and wireless phones.

SEVEN NIGHT

This can be a challenging placement for the Night person within the Earth week. The Night person, that likes to be secure and take things slowly and methodically, can find themselves jostled about by the bouncy, mental intensity of the Earth day sign. The conservative nature of the Night person may find Earth's intensity and mental fluctuations difficult to endure. This challenge to their mental well being may cause the Night person to become rigid in order to counteract the effects of the Earth influence. It is best for the Night person to be calm and take life easy and flow with life's ups and downs.

EIGHT SEED

For the Seed person, there will be many unexpected opportunities due to the placement within the Earth week. The combination of mental agility and the potential for financial success will be stimulated with this placement. It will also bring out the leadership qualities within the Seed person, giving them many ideals to bring to humanity.

The impact of Earth upon the famous Seed entertainer and role model, 8 Seed Bill Cosby, can be seen in his creative mind and ability to use different types of media to deliver his message of self esteem and accomplishment. He expressed his simple yet profound sense of family and strong values that are part of the Earth make-up.

NINE SERPENT

Backed by the empowering relationship between Serpent and Earth, the Serpent person will have many creative ideas. The charisma of the Serpent will be put to good use as the Earth day sign will motivate them to use their ideas and mental ability. The Serpent will find they can use spontaneity and inventiveness to their benefit.

The power of Serpent and Earth can be seen in the life of 9 Serpent Lilly Tomlin. Her natural charm combined with the mental ingenuity that the Earth day sign supplied can be seen in the wide variety of delightful characters that have made Lilly Tomlin famous.

TEN TRANSFORMER

With the help of the Earth day sign, the Transformer day sign will probably take on more mental interests then many Transformer people. The mental stimulation of Earth can support the Transformer person in their desires to take a more active part in the political situations of their community. The supportive relationship of Transformer and Earth can help the Transformer person to find many inventive and progressive ways to acquire wealth and help their community to prosper.

ELEVEN DEER

The artistic and sophisticated tastes of the Deer person can go through many challenges to get in touch with their true nature. They may be able to combine their love of travel with their interests, which will be stimulated by their assignment to the Earth week.

The challenges of the Deer to find and live their true selves can be seen in the life of the illustrious cook and television hostess, 11 Deer, Julia Child. It is fascinating to see how the Deer interest to wander through foreign countries and be productive combined with the Earth tendency toward the manifestation of innovative ideas. Her ability to turn her love of the foreign into ground-breaking work in creative cooking definitely had the mark of the Earth day sign upon it.

TWELVE STAR

The Star may come to shine in many unexpected ways if they are willing to stay on track and allow the Earth day sign to stimulate the creativity within them.

This is what happened to the renowned singer and Black musician, 12 Star Bo Diddley. The Earth influence even came out in his nickname: The Originator. He played a pivotal role in showing musicians new ideas about music that paved the way for the transition from Blues to Rock and Roll music. His innovative ideas about music influenced many 60's groups including The Rolling Stones and helped them bring a new musical sound to humanity.

THIRTEEN OFFERING

The help of the empowering relationship between the emotional and sometimes out of control Offering and the brilliant mind of Earth helped 13 Offering, James Taylor, find his way through a muddle of drugs and depression to become a song writer and singer. He had difficulty overcoming the emotional turmoil of the Offering day sign. Yet when stability and calm, which is so necessary to both Earth and Offering, came into his life, he was able to go on to write and sing. He became a 5 time Grammy winner and was inducted into the Rock and Roll Hall of Fame. The intensity of the number 13 can be seen in his life. This number brings out the most extreme aspect of any day sign. Yet with the empowering help of Earth, he has been able to triumph over his traumas and achieve world wide acclaim.

ONE DOG
COMMITMENT TO COMMUNITY

In The Mayan culture, as in most cultures, the day sign of Dog represents loyalty and service to others. The Dog personality will be very committed to a life style or group. This devotion to friends, family and community is the way the Dog day sign communicates their love. To be helpful fills the heart of the Dog day sign.

The day signs that come under the sway of the Dog week are 2 Monkey, 3 Road, 4 Reed, 5 Jaguar, 6 Eagle, 7 Wisdom, 8 Earth, 9 Flint, 10 Storm, 11 Sun, 12 Crocodile and 13 Wind.

TWO MONKEY

This interesting combination of mystery and surprise can suit the Monkey day sign to a tee. It is the unexpected that can give the Monkey day sign a new stage to perform on. As long as the Monkey can be flexible and use this energy to their advantage, the Monkey will be able to turn lemons into lemonade. Being positioned in this week will give Monkey more of an interest in settling down in a group of people. It might even help the Monkey to expand their focus to others, and not always see them as the center of the universe.

THREE ROAD

This is a challenging placement for the Road day sign. Both Road and Dog share a common interest. These two day signs are very dedicated to family and community. The Road day sign can become very committed to the group of people they are focused on, even if there are many challenges that come with this focus.

This allegiance to their community of choice can be seen in the life of 3 Road, Margaret Mead. As a cultural anthropologist, she became famous for her interest in the societies of Southeast Asia and the South Pacific. Her enthusiasm for the Dog's interest in the sexual practices of these cultures created a lot of conflict in the 1950's. She brought the ideas of sexual freedom to the Western world and is accredited with helping to start the sexual revolution of the 1960's. She was definitely expressing the Dog's love of sexuality and community.

FOUR REED

With the stimulation of the support of the Dog day sign, this Reed person will find acceptance for their ideas and beliefs. They will be able to find a community of supporters for their principles.

This is the case with the 4 Reed Jerry Brown, who was the governor of California and held other political posts as well. His dedication to his ideals of fiscal responsibility and environmental health brought him into controversy during his political career. The inflexibility of Reed worked for him as he became a crusader for his causes. He was able to use the Dog dedication to his state to bring financial health to California.

FIVE JAGUAR

The Dog day sign will help the Jaguar to come out of the underbrush and become involved in the life that is around them. With this placement, the Jaguar will be able to find loyalty and consistency in close relationships and community. The Jaguar day sign will also be motivated to use their healing and intuitive abilities for the benefit of not only the people in their lives but for the greater good as well.

SIX EAGLE

With this assignment to the Dog week, the Eagle personality will usually find that their plans for freedom will be unexpectedly compromised. They will be called into service for their community in ways that they are not able to foresee, even with the Eagle's ability for perceiving future possibilities.

The Dog day sign has many valuable lessons on loyalty and community that the Eagle born into this position in the Dog week, will have to learn. This may help the Eagle to have the family and relationships that all humans desire.

SEVEN WISDOM

Dedication to a cause or a goal will become even stronger within the Wisdom personality with this placement within the Dog week. Yet this dedication to family and goals may create oppositions and conflict for the quiet, sensitive Wisdom. This challenging assignment for Wisdom will spur them on to achieve their goals, no matter what personal challenges they have to overcome.

This is evidenced in the life of 7 Wisdom, Truman Capote, author and media personality. He is perhaps best known for his book, In Cold Blood. His Wisdom-like focus to pick clean the details of the story and present it from his perspective was a very harrowing and disturbing project. With Dog dedication he saw the 4 year project through to the end.

EIGHT EARTH

The support that Earth receives from the Dog day sign helps them to be part of a group and work for that group. Even though Earth people are not known for being team players, with the help of the Dog day sign, they will be very focused upon helping a larger group.

In the life of 39th president of the United States, 8 Earth Jimmy Carter, we can see that he had great dedication to the cause of human rights. His loyalty to this cause continued after his term of office was over. His innovative ideas, that came spewing out of this Earth person, motivated him to create new cabinet positions that addressed energy and education in government.

NINE FLINT

Backed by the power of the Dog day sign, this placement for Flint will help this day sign to achieve their goals. Flint represents the warrior energy, so this desire within the Flint personality may be enhanced. Fighting for a group that they believe in will also become strong within the Flint psyche.

This dedication to a cause or group can be seen in the life of Norman Vincent Peale. This crusader for positive thinking wrote books, did television and created organizations that upheld the values of freedom of worship.

TEN STORM

The loving, compassionate nature of the Storm personality will be in for some surprises from the Dog day sign. With this position, the Storm personality, that is very sympathetic, kind hearted and considerate, may find itself in situations that will unexpectedly allow these qualities to be brought to the world.

This is just what happened to the Storm born actor Jimmy Stewart, a 10 Storm. Whether he was acting in a comedy or a drama, his tender, caring personality always came though. It is just these qualities that propelled this easy going Storm person to the top of a field where his loving nature was communicated to generations.

ELEVEN SUN

With this place within the Dog week, the Sun day sign will be motivated to work for the cause of the people that they feel are important, no matter what the challenges.

This concept is evidenced within the life of the leader of the Soviet Union, 11 Sun Mikhail Gorbachev. In true Sun style, he was a benevolent ruler. He made many changes that brought more freedom to his suppressed people. With this challenging position within the Dog week, Mr. Gorbachev worked through great opposition to bring more freedom to his people.

TWELVE CROCODILE

The Dog day sign can be very helpful to the Crocodile person that falls into this placement. They may find themselves working in the areas of communication to help their extended family.

This positive support can be seen in the life of entertainer, 12 Crocodile, Bob Hope. With the help of the Dog day sign, the home body nature of Crocodile came out to shine in communication fields. One can see Mr. Hope's dedication to country, which is an extension of family and part of the Dog and Crocodile nature. His dedication to do what he could to uplift the soldiers that kept America safe during World War II and the conflicts that followed shows his loyalty to his country, his extended family.

THIRTEEN WIND

Even though this is an empowering position for the Wind day sign, it may cause the Wind person to alter their basic nature. The Wind person usually finds it hard to commit to relationship or community. With the help of the Dog day sign, the Wind person may be empowered to have a committed relationship and family. The Dog will help the Wind to settle down with those that this day sign finds helpful in their lives. Dog can also help Wind to focus on their communication and teaching abilities.

ONE NIGHT
SECURITY AND PRIVACY

This day sign has a very strong need to have secure foundations. It is also important for this day sign to feel safe and sound with their spiritual and intellectual beliefs as well as financial prosperity. They are also very reclusive. They have high standards that they will work very hard to achieve.

The day signs within the Night week are 2 Seed, 3 Serpent, 4 Transformer, 5 Deer, 6 Star, 7 Offering, 8 Dog, 9 Monkey, 10 Road, 11 Reed, 12 Jaguar and 13 Eagle.

TWO SEED

The Seed day sign is in a supportive environment within the Night week. Therefore, it is possible for the Seed to combine its natural desire for manifestation into areas of financial security. The Seed day sign, in this position, is serious, dedicated and focused on achieving their goals.

These qualities can be seen in the life of 2 Seed, Kirk Douglas, the legendary screen actor. He came from a poor family and was very dedicated to being successful in his life. He displayed the Seed attribute of leadership as well as the Night ability to take his work seriously and focus on his goals. He won many awards and has inspired many in the entertainment industry.

THREE SERPENT

Even though this is a challenging placement within the Night week, the Serpent day sign will be able to find a focus for their potent personal energies and desires. They may also be very emotional and will need a lot of seclusion and quiet time in order to keep in balance. This placement will motivate the Serpent to achieve security and financial stability. They may have very strong emotions and will need time away from others to allow their strong feelings to flow through them.

FOUR TRANSFORMER

This placement within the Night week can bring out many surprising attributes within the Transformer person. They may be very serious and also have a desire for upward mobility within their lives.

This can be seen in the life of Johann Wolfgang von Goethe. Aside from being an accomplished author, this German politician also had the Transformer inclination to take part in the affairs of his community. As a politician, he created more humane laws and carried out kinder sentences. He was in touch with the sub conscious, which is part of the Night nature. His writings in the fields of poetry, drama, music and philosophy inspired creativity in Europe for several generations.

FIVE DEER

With this empowering placement within the Night week, the imaginative and versatile Deer will find great encouragement. Even though the Night day sign may bring out the serious nature of Deer and possibly hinder their desire to roam the world, the connection that Deer and Night both have to the sub conscious, will motivate the Deer's mental creativity.

This can be seen in the life of Ian Fleming, the author who created the James Bond books. His espionage work in World War II, which is part of the Night focus on security, gave him the foundation for the 007 books that later became movies.

SIX STAR

With the support of Night, this position will bring stability and achievement to the Star day sign. This combination creates a very complex and somewhat off beat mind and personality.

These qualities can be seen in the life of comedian Jerry Lewis. Mr. Lewis has made a career with his wacky personality. The Night dedication to a focus can be seen in the amount of work that this renowned personality has brought to the world.

SEVEN OFFERING

The Offering person may find a lot of challenges with this placement within the Night week. The emotional nature of the Offering person will be challenged to find positive outlets with this placement. It is important for the Offering person to find socially acceptable ways to express their feelings. Otherwise they will have to work through many conflicts to find peace. With a good, stable family and living situation, that is inherent to the Night day sign, the Offering person will be able to find happiness.

EIGHT DOG

For the loyal and family oriented Dog day sign, there can be many surprises in store with this position within the Night week. These people can make great leaders and support their community in many unexpected ways.

The element of surprise can be seen in the life of celebrated Country music star Willie Nelson. Willy was in for a big surprise when he found that his accounting firm, Price Waterhouse had not paid his taxes and he owed the IRS 32 million dollars in 1990. He has also had a few other surprises from time to time, but he has done a great job of bringing the music of his community, Country music, to a world-wide audience.

NINE MONKEY

The empowering support of the Night day sign will help this Monkey to shine. With the help of Night, the Monkey's natural abilities to be imaginative and be the center of attention will be amplified.

The help of the Night day sign to stay focused and pursue their goals can be seen in the life of actor Dustin Hoffman. Mr. Hoffman has been able to use his playful Monkey ability to take on many diverse roles. The wide variety of roles that Mr. Hoffman has played is a testimony to the skill and versatility of the Monkey day sign.

TEN ROAD

In this supportive placement, the easy going Road personality will be able to honor the Night desire to be successful and achieve prosperity. Both Night and Road are interested in manifesting abundance in all areas of life. With the help of the Night day sign, Road people will be able to stick to their goals and achieve a great deal for themselves and the ones that they love.

ELEVEN REED

Even though this is a challenging position for a Reed person, the Night day sign will give the Reed determination, endurance and commitment to what they want to achieve. The Reed person will be spurred on by the Night day sign to use their full potential.

This is powerfully illustrated in the life of the 32nd president of the United States, Franklin D. Roosevelt. Mr. Roosevelt faced an incredible amount of challenges during his political career. Politics and high ideals are part of the Reed nature. With the help of the Night perseverance, he became governor of New York and later president of the United States. While crippled by polio, he led the United States through the most challenging of times: World War II. The Night day sign worked with him to help him regenerate the economy after the great depression.

TWELVE JAGUAR

This placement of Jaguar within the Night week can give the Jaguar the perseverance it needs to use its mental ability to the fullest.

This can be seen in the life of the famed inventor Henry Ford. The steady focus of Henry Ford to manifest his technical ideas led him to invent the automobile and also create race cars and airplanes. He is credited with inventing the assembly line and with giving workers good wages. He focused his attention on the community of his workers and gave them a good standard of life. He illustrates the Night's desire to achieve.

THIRTEEN EAGLE

This is an empowering position for the Eagle day sign. They are able to see the potentials that are available to them and then get the help of the Night focus and determination to achieve their visions.

Merv Griffin, best known as a television game show creator, made his start as a singer and actor on the stage. He had the Eagle's foresight to see that television had great potential. He was able to make great contributions to the field of entertainment by using his Eagle's vision of future potentials and the Night perseverance.

ONE WISDOM
REGENERATION AND DEDICATION

The Wisdom day sign is very serious and concerned with material life. This makes them very interested in achieving status through hard work. They have very high standards that they are able to achieve and expect others to do the same. They are interested in releasing what no longer is useful.

The day signs under the influence of the Wisdom day sign are 2 Earth, 3 Flint, 4 Storm, 5 Sun, 6 Crocodile, 7 Wind, 8 Night, 9 Seed, 10 Serpent, 11 Transformer, 12 Deer and 13 Star.

TWO EARTH

This day sign can take the many incredible ideas that come spewing forth from its fertile mind and bring them into manifestation with the help of the grounded and dedicated nature of the Wisdom influence.

Looking into the life of Thomas Jefferson, the 3rd President of the United States, we can see that all the Earth ideas were able to manifest with the help of the Wisdom's dedication. The Wisdom day sign helped this Earth person rise to the top, administer to others and see his ideas come to fruition.

THREE FLINT

The challenge and strengthening connection between Wisdom and Flint can spur the Flint person on to achieve great success. The Flint day sign already has the desire to work hard for a cause. The Flint will find great motivation with the Wisdom's support. Being that this is a challenging position for the Flint success will probably come after struggle.

This can be seen in the life of politician Gary Hart. Mr. Hart was running for president of the United States when a scandal over an affair with Donna Rice caused him to drop out of the race. Even with all the challenges he faced, he has still been able to work in politics. His focus, true to the warrior energy of Flint, has been homeland security.

FOUR STORM

With the support of the Wisdom day sign, this placement of Storm will get help in expressing it's creativity in a positive way. The Wisdom desire to work independently will also help this playful, youth oriented day sign be successful in unique and inspiring ways.

The life of the children's author Dr. Seuss is a classic example of what Storm and Wisdom can achieve together. The humorous and loving qualities of the Dr. Seuss books, movies and television specials have spread the Storm childlike playfulness to children around the world.

FIVE SUN

Being that Wisdom is an empowering influence for the creative energies of the multitalented Sun, it is not surprising that the focus and determination of Wisdom will help this artistic day sign rise to the top of any field of creative endeavor.

The potential of Sun and Wisdom can be seen in the singer and songwriter, Bruce Springsteen. This icon of Americana has risen to the top of his profession. A crowning achievement was his performance at the Inaugural celebration of President Barack Obama.

SIX CROCODILE

With this position within the Wisdom week, the Crocodile may find themselves in unfamiliar situations do to their mystery and surprise relationship. Wisdom and Crocodile do share an interest in working hard. Yet the Crocodile is not usually interested in climbing up the ladder of success.

By utilizing the help of the Wisdom day sign, this Crocodile may find that unexpected opportunities for achievement will come to them. It is important that the Crocodile not allow their tendency to dominate others take over when they are in administrative positions.

SEVEN WIND

These two day signs, Wisdom and Wind, have a challenging bond. The Wisdom demands consistency and dedication to achievement. The Wind person likes to flit from situation to situation. The Wisdom day sign will most likely manifest situations where the Wind person will have to focus on goals. Even though events will occur that the Wind person may not enjoy, they will see as they surrender to the opportunities that Wisdom provides, that single-mindedness in manifesting success will pay off.

EIGHT NIGHT

Wisdom smiles upon and supports the Night person in many areas of life. Both Night and Wisdom are very attainment oriented. Both of these day signs will work hard to achieve financial prosperity and security.

Wisdom will probably cause the Night person to be dragged out of their cavern so that they can claim the potential that is within them. Due to the supportive nature of this connection, this day sign will probably enjoy the opportunities that are presented to them.

NINE SEED

The force of Wisdom is empowering this placement of Seed to reach the height of its potential. In areas of financial prosperity and leadership, the Wisdom will assist Seed in rising to the top of their profession. The serious nature of Wisdom will keep this Seed day sign in line so that they can focus on attainment.

The leadership potential of the Seed has been brought to the height of accomplishment in the life of Henry Kissinger. This politician has made incredible contributions to world government and policies and has received the Nobel Peace Prize.

TEN SERPENT

The dynamic, imaginative nature of Serpent is given focus and application within the Wisdom week. This is a mystery and surprise placement, so the Serpent will probably just be doing what they usually do and will be surprised at the achievement that they will attain.

This can be seen in the life of Country singer, songwriter and actor Gene Autry. He brought his passion for Country music to the world during the 1930's. With his Serpent drive to manifest his imaginative creations and the Wisdom nose to the grindstone, his prolific career touched the field of music, movie making and even baseball. He manifested all his passions in a spectacular way.

ELEVEN TRANSFORMER

Even though this is a challenging position for the Transformer person, it can bring out the best in the Transformer day sign. Both Wisdom and Transformer have the desire to work hard for a cause. The Transformer ability to work with money and property combined with the Wisdom desire for accomplishment can benefit the Transformer person.

An example of this can be seen in the life of financial advisor Paul Volcker. The attraction of the Transformer person to gold, the riches of the underworld, is evidenced in Mr. Volker's career. He was Chairman of the Federal Reserve under Presidents Carter and Reagan and had the position of Chairman of the Economic Recovery Board under President Obama.

TWELVE DEER

The fun loving, meandering Deer will find support from the Wisdom day sign for all their endeavors. The Deer person will be able to bring their interest in art and personal expression to the height of their potential with the dedication of the Wisdom day sign.

The life of Steve Allen, a writer, comedian, author and composer is evidence that with Wisdom giving you support, one can achieve greatness in your lifetime. Steve Allen hosted the I've Got a Secret, The Tonight Show and What's My Line television shows. These programs satisfied his curiosity and the Deer desire to explore and find new and interesting life situations.

THIRTEEN STAR

This position within the Wisdom week will help the notorious Star person to be able to express their views and ideals in a commanding way. The Star perchance for controversy will be strengthened and heightened to its potential with the help of Wisdom's dedication and drive.

The career of George Orwell, the political writer who penned the books 1984 and Animal Farm was able to challenge dictatorial governmental ideals. He spoke out against social injustice and totalitarianism. The Star love of debate was used in a profound way. This writer that is still within the minds of people today.

ONE OFFERING
THE POWER OF EMOTION AND IMAGINATION

The Offering day sign has deep seeded passions and urges. They have a leaning toward intuition. They can be overcome by irrational behavior if they are not able to keep their intense motivations in check. When they harness the power within them, they can be great leaders, psychics and performers.

The day signs under the authority of the Offering day sign are
2 Dog, 3 Monkey, 4 Road, 5 Reed, 6 Jaguar, 7 Eagle, 8 Wisdom, 9 Earth, 10 Flint, 11 Storm, 12 Sun and 13 Crocodile.

TWO DOG

The Dog day sign will find that they have support for their interests and passions with this place within the Offering week. The passionate nature of the Offering day sign will probably intensity Dog's interest in sexual expression.

The support of the Offering day sign will also amplify the Dog's interest in leadership. This Dog person's natural helpfulness will probably be energized. This may cause the Dog person to take an active part in the affairs of his "pack" or community. Loyalty issues will also be intensified with this placement.

THREE MONKEY

The bouncy, fun loving Monkey will probably be more captivating then the usual Monkey person. The Monkey love of the spotlight will be intensified and will probably cause many problems for the Monkey person, due to the challenging nature of this position.

These Monkey people may have an uncompromising streak within them. They may also find that they get so carried away with their feelings that they may tend to neglect responsibilities. Hopefully this Monkey person will have a partner that will help them keep on track.

FOUR ROAD

The Offering day sign will bring surprises and has a powerful destiny waiting for this humble Road person. The passion of the Offering day sign and the unexpected controversial nature of his career can be seen in the life of Playboy impresario Hugh Hefner.

Mr. Hefner was just following his passions, as the Offering day sign would have him do and he ran into great opposition with his new ideas of sexual freedom. The shock of his first wife's affair paved the way for permissiveness that condoned Hugh's promiscuity. This shocking event in his life has led to his sexual beliefs and his media empire.

FIVE REED

The Reed person will be able to rise to the height of their potential with this empowering position in the

Offering week. With the help of the Offering day sign, the Reed will have passion behind their ideals and theories. These Reed people will be able to find accomplishment with the help of the Offering day sign.

One thing to remember is that the usually rigid Reed will find that they will be swayed by their strong emotions that are part of the Offering psyche. If the Reed person does not get involved in trying to dominate others with their ideals, they will find acceptance and success.

SIX JAGUAR

The interest in money and finance, that is natural to the Jaguar day sign, will find great support from the Offering day sign. Even though the Jaguar is not naturally a public person, the passion of the Offering day sign will motivate the Jaguar to come out into the world. The Jaguar will be able to use their natural ability to connect with the riches of the earth to the benefit of all.

This potential can be seen in the life of the financier J.P. Morgan. Mr. Morgan had an interest in steel and gold, which are naturally attracted to Jaguars. He started U.S. Steel Corporation. His interest in steel also became useful in starting railroad companies. In 1893 and 1907 Morgan was able to use his expertise with gold to avoid panic and collapse of the U. S. Treasury.

SEVEN EAGLE

True to the Eagle's need for freedom and expression, this placement within the Offering week will breed highly independent people that will be at the forefront of new trends. They also have a keen appreciation of the arts, especially music.

These traits are clearly evidenced in the life of the Beatle's drummer Ringo Starr. He was in the middle of the most progressive musical group in history. His unique drumming style created a new paradigm for drummers to have a greater part in a band's composition and style. His need for freedom dominated and Ringo went on to do his own work after the Beatles separated.

EIGHT WISDOM

The emotions of the Offering day sign are expressed within the Wisdom day sign in many unusual ways. The usually serious nature of Wisdom can combine with Offering's ardor and appeal to create a truly unique individual.

This can be seen in the life of Country music artist Patsy Cline. Country music was the perfect outlet for this Wisdom's melancholy perspective on life. The intensity of her voice and the emotions she expressed made great use of the combination of Wisdom and Offering. Like the surprise relationship of Wisdom and Offering, her death was an unexpected surprise. Her plane crash shocked millions that saw her flame extinguished too soon.

NINE EARTH

With this empowering placement within the Offering week, the Earth day sign will be able to take advantage of the help that Offering can give them to accomplish greatness. The myriad of ideas that come forth from the Earth person will find acceptance and usefulness in their chosen field.

This is evidenced in the life of behaviorist and social philosopher B.F. Skinner .He created new fields within the discipline of Psychology and has been touted as the most influential psychologist of the 20th century.

TEN FLINT

The supportive connection between Flint and Offering can bring out the emotions in the Flint person. If these emotions are directed in the proper way, they can add a layer of sentiment to the usually stoic Flint.

If not kept in balance, the Flint can get out of control. This can be seen in the life of the Italian dictator of World War II, Benito Mussolini. He started out using his passion for the benefit of his country. He made a lot of progressive changes for Italy. He was influenced by Hitler's zeal that fueled his own lust for power. This out of control fanaticism brought disaster to his country in the end.

ELEVEN STORM

The challenging relationship between Offering and Storm can lead the intuitive and good natured Storm person into very intense spiritual and psychic experiences. This placement can bring out the connection to the sub conscious for the sensitive Storm person.

This can be evidenced in the life of the controversial psychic, medium and founder of the Theosophical Society, Madam Helena Blavatsky. She was a pioneer in many ways and broke through the many challenges that confronted her to bring new ideas on spirituality and past lives to Western society.

TWELVE SUN

The relationship of surprise for the Sun/Offering day sign combination can work in many mysterious ways. The kingly Sun can suffer from the intense emotions of Offering that cause them to be overly sensitive and more idealistic then other Suns. This creates problems in relationships as the Sun person will have drives that they will find hard to repress. This placement may give the Sun person an intense temper.

This can be seen in the life of Ian Xel Lungold, the creator of the Mayan Calendar and Conversion Codex and lecturer on the Mayan Calendar. I can definitely say, having lived and worked with Ian for 2 years that he did have problems with relationships and a very intense temper. It was his temper that ultimately led to his demise.

THIRTEEN CROCODILE

This empowering yet intense placement of Crocodile combined with the number 13 can create a person that can use the power of both Crocodile and Offering in a big way. The combination of Crocodile and Offering will produce a person with very strong instincts and emotions. These people may be dominating, but they are liked by many.

The comedian John Cleese is a 13 Crocodile who got out of the Crocodile swamp and went into the spotlight through his somewhat extreme brand of comedy. His work with the group Monty Python created many intensely disgusting images that brought great emotional release through laughter to millions of people.

ONE WIND
COMMUNICATION AND CHANGE

This day sign is focused on communication and the realm of mental ideas. Often those born to a Wind day sign can be very interested in all types of knowledge. They may be teachers or communicate information in some way. The changeable or what I call the fickle aspect of Wind can be very disconcerting. They may be passionate about a situation and then abruptly change their mind and go in another direction.

Those day signs under the reign of Wind are 2 Night, 3 Seed, 4 Serpent, 5 Transformer, 6 Deer, 7 Star, 8 Offering, 9 Dog, 10 Monkey, 11 Road, 12 Reed and 13 Jaguar.

TWO NIGHT

This day sign has a great ability to communicate the ideas of the sub conscious. The combination of the Night person's connection to the sub conscious and the Wind focus on ideas and mental concepts can bring out powerful expression from the inner regions of the psyche.

The life of Joseph Campbell, who brought the power of the subconscious out to express itself in mythology, is a classic example of the combination of the potential of Night and Wind. Mr. Campbell was definitely affected by the Wind desire to communicate. This is evidenced in the many volumes he wrote. With the Wind's help he expressed the Night's connection to the subconscious and the information stored within.

THREE SEED

The need for artistic expression that mirrors their own unique being is very powerful within the mind of this Seed person. The nature of Seed people, to express their uniqueness through communication can be seen in the life of singer and song writer, Grace Slick.

She came into prominence during the time when another renowned Seed singer, Jim Morrison was also expressing himself. The Seed tendency toward sexual expression can be seen in Grace Slick's life. The Wind influence is evidenced by her songs communicating her political ideas. Her negative communication to police also got her into a lot of trouble.

FOUR SERPENT

This is a supportive placement for the Serpent. The help of the Wind day sign will cause the primal nature of the Serpent to become more communicative. With the help of Wind, the Serpent will probably be able to express the fluid, hypnotic movement of the Serpent in some verbal or literary way.

The Serpent's dynamic magnetism may propel them into leadership positions. This should be good for the Serpent person. The positive nature of this connection of Wind and Serpent will most likely give the Serpent the ability to communicate effectively to those that follow or are influenced by them.

FIVE TRANSFORMER

For the Transformer person, this is an empowering placement. Transformer will be able to be more expressive. This ability to communicate effectively is doubled, because these day signs are both ruled by the direction of the North, where ideas manifest.

This tendency may cause the Transformer person to take a more active part in leadership then most Transformer people. On the other hand, the Wind influence may cause the Transformer person to change their mind a great deal before they firmly set their mind on a course of action.

SIX DEER

The element of surprise and destiny will be very strong within the life of this Deer person. This can be evidenced within the life of novelist James Michener. The Deer tendency to travel the world came to Mr. Michener unexpectedly. His stint in the U.S. Navy during WWII was the impetus that started his prolific writing career. His most famous novels, Hawaii, Tales of the South Pacific (turned into the broadway musical and movie South Pacific) and Sayonara all stemmed from the Deer love of foreign cultures and the Wind love of communication.

SEVEN STAR

The challenging nature of this placement within the Wind week may bring the Star person into a great deal of controversy. This position within the Wind week will bring out the desire to debate or communicate unpopular concepts.

This situation can be seen in the life of actor and social activist Ed Asner. Wind and Star worked together in his life to bring him into an area of career that gave him a platform from which to get recognition. His public renown gave him the perfect podium to present his political views. Mr. Asner has suffered because of his political views. His very popular television show, Lou Grant, was canceled due to his political ideas. Even though Mr. Asner has faced many challenges to his political expression, he has not been silenced.

EIGHT OFFERING

Even though this is a supportive placement for the Offering person, the combination of Offering and Wind may bring about some difficult tendencies within the Offering person. The Offering person will probably take on the Wind's volatile personality. This position within the Wind week may stimulate the Offering desire to express their emotions verbally.

If the Offering person can keep their emotions under control, they will be able to utilize the communication abilities of Wind to enhance their leadership abilities. Consistency may be hard for the Offering person, due to the Wind's changeable nature.

NINE DOG

With the empowering connection between Dog and Wind, the Dog person will find that their ability to communicate effectively will be enhanced.

The life of the writer Samuel Clemens, better known as Mark Twain, exemplifies the blending of Wind and Dog in a positive, productive light. Mark Twain became famous for his descriptions of his territory, the Southern United States. His playful Dog humor and love of the South brought a lot of healing wit to the world.

TEN MONKEY

This placement within the Wind week can bring many surprises to the Monkey person. This is what happened to the actress Maureen O'Hara. Her acting career was almost doomed to failure at the start, due to bad make-up and costume for her first film test. Fate stepped in and her seemingly unsuccessful test was seen by the actor Charles Laughton, He helped Maureen live up to her potentials of a versatile Monkey performer. The mystery/surprise relationship with the Wind day sign worked for her. It gave her the opportunity to communicate and use her Monkey desire for attention into a diverse career

ELEVEN ROAD

The challenges that will beset the Road person in this placement will not stop them from completing their goals. This is the case with famous Road person J. Edgar

Hoover, the founder of the Federal Bureau of Investigation.

Mr. Hoover exhibited the down side of the Road personality. He kept his feeing bottled up and then took them out on people under him. The Wind temper expressed itself through this Road person by his tendency to personalize his punishment of people that displeased him. The challenge to bring law and order to the wild and corrupt 1930's shows the Road's ability to persevere to achieve a goal.

TWELVE REED

The supportive connection between Wind and Reed can help the Reed person communicate their political ideals and beliefs in a big way. This is demonstrated in the life of political activist Ralph Nader. The insightful and deep thinking of the Reed nature was able to be expressed with the help of the Wind day sign.

Mr. Nader has contributed to sharing important knowledge with the public about consumerism, environmental tribulations and humanitarian problems. His ability to reveal problems in many areas of life has received support from many who believe in his causes. The people called Nader's Raiders enabled many publications of social and political injustice to come to public attention.

THIRTEEN JAGUAR

With the muscle of the Wind behind this Jaguar person, great things can be accomplished. The Jaguar connection to what the Maya call the underworld, or what we in the Western world call the subconscious, is evidenced in the life of Edgar Cayce.

Mr. Cayce's life is a clear illustration of the Jaguar's ability to journey into the realms of the sub conscious to help others heal and to reveal information. The number 13 validates that Mr. Cayce was the ultimate representation of the Jaguar ability to journey to the realms of the sub conscious.

He was able to document a vast number of his readings with the help of people to record them. This documentation of his work has caused Mr. Cayce to be thought of as the founder of the New Age movement of spiritual thought. He is the most renown psychic of our time.

ONE EAGLE
THE BIG PICTURE AND THE FINE PRINT

Two of the qualities of the Eagle day sign are that they have the ability to see a grand perspective of events and potentials. With this ability to see the big picture, Eagles are also good at details. They desire their freedom to fly, but may make sacrifices to stay happy in a nest with others.

The day signs born into the Eagle week are 2 Wisdom, 3 Earth, 4 Flint, 5 Storm, 6 Sun, 7 Crocodile, 8 Wind, 9 Night, 10 Seed, 11 Serpent, 12 Transformer, and 13 Deer.

TWO WISDOM

This is a supportive position for the Wisdom day sign. Wisdom can find practical applications for the vision of the future that that the Eagle offers. The ability to utilize this perspective can help the Wisdom take advantage of future trends and profit from them.

The practical applications of futuristic visions can be seen in the life of science fiction writer Ray Bradbury. He was a prolific writer that produced famous books such as the Martian Chronicles and The Illustrated Man. His work paved the way for the growth of science fiction books, movies and television shows.

THREE EARTH

There are trials in store for those born into this position of Earth within the Eagle week. Even though this can cause the Earth person to face many challenges, the influence of the Eagle can bring many new dimensions into the mind of the Earth person.

The natural ability of the Earth person to have many thoughts and ideas can be enhanced with the far reaching vision that the Eagle gives. The Earth person will most likely come up with ideas that have useful applications.

FOUR FLINT

Mystery and surprise will be the key note for the Flint person who is born within the Eagle week. The sphere of thought, that is powerful for the Flint person, will be enhanced by this placement within the Eagle week. These Flint people will most likely have ideas that are far reaching.

This can be seen in the life of Alfred Adler, who has been considered one of the founding fathers, along with Sigmund Freud and Carl Jung, of modern psychology. Adler had the far reaching vision to speak of the inferiority complex and was an advocate for feminism.

FIVE STORM

Backed by the empowering connection between Eagle and Storm, this position of Storm will be able to be successful in areas where long term planning and attention to details will come in handy.

The Storm person will find that they will be able to blend the Eagle's need for freedom with the Storm's desire to have committed relationships. The outcome may be that this Storm person will have unusual relationships.

These unique relationships, that may not follow the guidelines of our social traditions, will allow them to have deep connections yet personal freedom to explore the world.

SIX SUN

This is a supportive placement for this Sun. With the help of the far sighted Eagle, this Sun will be able to use their innate ability to lead others with foresight and compassion.

This can be seen in the life of Gerald Ford, the 38th president and 40th Vice President of the United States of America. Mr. Ford ascended to these positions of power after Richard Nixon was impeached and Spiro Agnew resigned. He displayed the kindness of a benevolent authority figure when he pardoned Richard Nixon and helped end the war in Viet Nam. He was well liked and appreciated for his endeavors at leading our nation during difficult times of economic and social unrest.

SEVEN CROCODILE

The Eagle will bring challenges into the life of the stay at home Crocodile. There may be conflicts for this placement of Crocodile. The Crocodile wants to stay home, raise a family and oversee their lair. The Eagle, on the other hand, wants to see the world, be free of attachments and explore.

As you can see, the Crocodile person will be dealing with this dichotomy throughout their lives. It is important for the Crocodile person to find balance between these two contradictory tendencies to find happiness and fulfillment in life.

EIGHT WIND

The combination of the Wind's mental ability and the Eagle's foresight and long range vision combined nicely in the life of the 33rd president of the United States, Harry S. Truman.

The element of surprise played a big part in Mr. Truman's life. He ascended to the office of president after the death of Franklin Delano Roosevelt in 1945. His great ideas of the Berlin airlift and the founding of NATO, are a few of the projects that he created. He was able to use the mental creativity of Wind and the vision of the Eagle to produce changes in government that are still here today.

NINE NIGHT

This is a placement for Night that will be empowering. It will help the reclusive Night person come out of their cave and take action in the world. The Night person will probably use this ability to create security and stability in their lives.

This can be seen in the life of the creator of the long running show on television, American Bandstand. Dick Clark was able to use the Night tendency for financial prosperity to turn American Bandstand into a profitable situation for himself, even after he left the show as the host.

He used his Eagle ability to see future potential by becoming involved with game shows such as the $10,000

Pyramid. The game show Jeopardy brought him prosperity and many awards.

TEN SEED

With the support of the Eagle day sign, this placement of Seed will find success and appreciation within their lives. The Eagle day sign will support the Seed in being themselves and being known for their unique personality.

The life of film star Greta Garbo is a good example of the tendency of the Seed person to manifest a unique persona. Ms. Garbo became a film legend that revolved around her desire for Eagle-like freedom and seclusion. She was chased by paparazzi who wanted to take pictures of her until the day she died.

ELEVEN SERPENT

This Serpent ended up in a challenging position in the Eagle week. This may cause the serpent to have a difficult time in manifesting their personal expression. They may not be given the appreciation they deserve.

This can be seen in the life of author Herman Melville. Mr. Melville was not given the admiration that his works deserved during his lifetime. His novel Moby Dick was acclaimed as one of the masterpieces of American and world literature some thirty years after his death.

TWELVE TRANSFORMER

This placement within the Eagle week can bring many surprises and unexpected twists and turns into the life of the Transformer person. The Eagle will motivate the Transformer person to go against their natural tendency to focus their lives on family and community.

The Eagle's need for freedom will possibly bring some unplanned events into the Transformer person's life. It is important for the Transformer person to find a way to blend the two seemingly contradictory desires for freedom and family in their lives.

THIRTEEN DEER

With Eagle empowering the Deer person, there may be a strong need for freedom within this Deer person. It is already within the Deer nature to roam and be free. With the guidance of Eagle, this person will most likely have an unusual occupation that will cause them to travel and have many new experiences.

It is possible for the Deer person to find happiness within relationships, but it must be a situation that will accommodate their desire to be free to experience the beauty of the planet. The Deer person will most likely have an occupation that affords opportunities to travel and experiences of art and culture.

ONE STAR
COMPETITION AND MENTAL AGILITY

The Star love of challenge and debate can bring altercation to the lives of those born within this week. The Star's mental skills and desire to stand up for their point of view can lead the day signs born into this week into many interesting confrontations.

The day signs affected by the Star ruler of this week are 2 Offering, 3 Dog, 4 Monkey, 5 Road, 6 Reed, 7 Jaguar, 8 Eagle, 9 Wisdom, 10 Earth, 11 Flint, 12 Storm and 13 Sun.

TWO OFFERING

This day sign will have many surprises in store for them. They are in a mystery/surprise relationship with Star. The Offering tendency to have strong emotions and the Star love of presenting their ideas to the world can have a positive or negative effect.

For the late movie actor, George C. Scott, the Star influence was a positive one. He is most famous for his roles that portray military conflict. His roles in Stanley Kubrick's Dr. Strange Love and Patton reflect his own military career and the Star love of facing adversity.

THREE DOG

This challenging placement for the Dog person can bring about confrontation. this will stimulate the placid Dog to take a greater role in leadership or other areas where stepping up to the plate is necessary.

This can be difficult for the Dog person. This challenge may bring out the best in the Dog personality and help them to use their abilities in a leadership or other areas of authority. The Dog person may not enjoy being thrust into the spotlight, but they will do their best.

FOUR MONKEY

This is the perfect position for the Monkey person to shine. They will come to places of prominence with the support of the Star day sign. The Monkey person is very clever in this placement and can play a variety of roles with no difficulty.

This is easy to see in the life of the kidnapped heiress Patty Hearst. She went from victim to soldier in the Symbionese Liberation Army with ease. Whether she realized it or not, as a Monkey, she loved the attention and turned it into a pseudo career.

FIVE ROAD

With the power of the Star day sign behind them, this placement of Road can achieve a great deal. The humble nature of Road will get an ego boost from the self-centered Star day sign.

This can be seen in the life of the low-key but very powerful 5 star general in World War II and United States president, Dwight D. Eisenhower. Mr. Eisenhower seemed to thrive on the Star's love of conflict and the need to be right. He entered politics to counter the non-interventionism of Robert Taft and wanted his war against Communism to prevail.

SIX REED

This position within the Star week can cause the Reed person to fight for the ideas and principles that they feel are important. Usually the Reed person will be happy just presenting their ideas to friends and family.
With the motivation of the Star day sign, this Reed person may unexpectedly find themselves in the middle of public debates, supporting the ideas that they feel are important. The Reed person may be in for a lot of Star surprises.

SEVEN JAGUAR

This is a challenging position for Jaguar. The quiet Jaguar may be motivated to come out of the bushes and stand up for what they believe in. This will not be an easy road for the Jaguar to walk, but they can achieve greatness in their area of expertise if they allow the Star day sign to help them.

This is clearly evidenced in the life of the "trash talking", loud mouthed, controversy-loving boxer, Muhammad Ali. It is easy to see the Star influence in Ali's life. He is probably best known for his arrogant, conceited speeches before his fights. The Star day sign was having fun with him and helped him get out to the Jaguar undergrowth and shine like a Star!

EIGHT EAGLE

With the support of the Star day sign, the Eagle can fly high and obtain a position of status. The Eagle day sign is usually not attracted to the spotlight or to confrontation. Most Eagles will take being alone over conflict with others.

Even so, with the help of the Star day sign, the Eagle may find prominence in areas that they find attractive. The Star day sign will motivate the Eagle to speak up and not fly away when they are faced with conflict. The Star day sign will help the Eagle fight for their goals and what they feel is right.

NINE WISDOM

The dynamic and versatile actor Marlon Brando is an example of what can be achieved when a day sign is placed into a week that is empowering. Mr. Brando is noted for his mumbling, almost reclusive style of his role in Francis Ford Coppola's the Godfather movies. This role personified the Wisdom's humble, low key persona, yet has the Star's love of power and authority.

The Star day sign propelled this Wisdom person into the position of being one of the most influential actors of the 20th century.

TEN EARTH

This placement of the mentally spewing nature of Earth within the Star week can bring many surprises to this day sign. The Earth person is naturally expressive of their ideas.

The Earth person may not want to find conflict, but as they naturally express their ideas, they may experience unexpected responses. With this position, the Earth day sign really needs to think before they churn out their ideas to those around them. They may be surprised at the reactions that they get!

ELEVEN FLINT

Even though this is a challenging placement for the Flint person, it has not been a problem but a motivation for the pop rock star Britney Spears. Her Flint ability to write and communicate can be seen in her many extremely successful albums and tours. She has the mental ability to diversify her business interests and has owned restaurants, created fragrance lines and acting on television shows.

The tendency of overindulgence within the Star day sign can be seen in her excessive use of drugs that resulted in the loss of her children. The over the top tendency of the Star day sign is very evident in her life.

TWELVE STORM

This day sign gets a lot of support from the Star. The creativity and connection to the sub conscious that is strong within the Storm person can come to the surface and be expressed with the help of the Star day sign.

This is what happened in the life of Storm person Peter Sellers. The Star day sign helped him find a means of expression for his active and brilliant imagination.

Unfortunately, the Star tendency for over indulgence can also be seen in Mr. Sellers private life. He had a dream – like life style that floated into many areas of the subconscious. The Star's excesses with drug abuse also created many problems in his life.

THIRTEEN SUN

The empowering nature of the Sun day sign within the Star week can bring about a great deal of notoriety for this person. This Sun will most likely be able to maintain and present the words or other information in a positive way.

This can be witnessed in the life of British writer Alan Watts, who brought the Eastern philosophy to a Western world. He was able to take the knowledge of Buddhism and, with the Star influence, give his own slant on the teachings which have made them more digestible to people in modern society.

THREE STEP SYSTEM FOR HARMONIZING WITH THE TZOLKIN

Now that you have discovered the meaning behind your Mayan astrology day sign and number and week you were born into, you are ready to become more involved with the Tzolkin and the Mayan astrology system. I have created a three step method for aligning with the knowledge that the Tzolkin has to offer.

The energy that is emitted from the Galactic Center or the center of our Milky Way affects us just as the energy from the planets in our solar system affects us

The following steps can be used to help you synchronize with the Tzolkin and the energy that is emitted from the core of our universe.

Do as many steps as your life can accommodate at this time. Don't feel guilty if you cannot do all the steps mentioned here. Simply putting your attention on your day sign will align you with the frequency of the Galactic Center, the creator energy or what the Maya call the Hu Nab Ku.

STEP ONE

Learn your day sign and number and the week you were born in. Look at your symbol. The visual representation of the Mayan glyph for your day sign will open you up to the energy that your day sign and its number represent.

Along with the visual representation of the day sign, the number and name of the day sign and day sign

230

of your birth week also have energy to give you. Ancient languages do have power. I have put the Kiche' Maya name for the day signs in the book. I feel that the Kiche' Maya name is probably the purist representation of the energy of the name, even though the Yucatec Maya names for the day signs are the most widely used. Use the name that appeals to you most or is easiest for you to pronounce. Both names have power.

When you look at your symbol and number while repeating the name, you will create a resonance with the day sign that will start the synchronization process. Don't be too concerned if you do not pronounce the name properly. What you will think and feel about your day sign may change as time goes by. Any connection to the ancient Mayan dialects will develop within you as you continue to look at your day sign symbol, number and think the name.

Have the drawing of your day sign and the number accessible to you where you may see it during your day if possible. That will be all that is really needed to harmonize with the Galactic Center.

Finally, it is also important to think upon the direction that rules your day sign. The direction of your day sign will give you more information about yourself. My day sign's direction is the North, the color white. The area of the North is focused on the mind, communication, and travel. The day signs that are ruled by the South, and have the color yellow, are focused on the body. This also means tangible, practical aspects of material life. The day signs ruled by the direction of the East, signified by the color of red, are very energetic and are good initiators of projects. Those day signs ruled by the

West, and are connected to the color blue, are good at completion, retrospection, intuition and regeneration.

The personality of the day sign, the number, ruler of your birth week and the direction all come together to give you the essence of your potentials, inclinations and strengths. If you allow yourself to acknowledge this potential of your being, you will begin to resonate with the energy that emits from the Hu Nab Ku.

STEP TWO: FOLLOWING EACH NEW MAYAN WEEK

The next phase of attuning to the Tzolkin will be to actually follow the days and weeks of the Tzolkin and pay attention to the energy of each new day. With the charts you will be able to keep track of what day today is.

This is something that you might do at the beginning of your day. Once you have visually and mentally connected with the day sign and direction of the day, you will have a sense of how the day will affect you personally. You will have an awareness of how the energy of the day intermingles with your personal energy.

Is today a challenge day for you? Is it a supportive day for you? Understanding how your direction (North, South, East or West) interacts with the direction of the present day will give you insights on how to put this day to work for yourself. Each day has the potential to be a good day, if you use the energy of the present day properly. Acknowledge the presence of what you might think of as the visiting day sign that is taking dominance for this day. Then think about how your personal day sign is affected by the energy of the present day.

If the day sign of the present day is **supportive or empowering**, you may be able to use that energy to find nurturing or help with aspects of life. Supportive days are good times to take off, nurture yourself, and be around people that nurture you. An empowering day is a good time to interact with people in business or personal situations.

When the present day is **challenging to you**, it is really a good time to break through stagnant situations. I have found that many stagnant situations have been resolved, of their own accord, on my challenge days. If the stagnation is not resolved, then it is not the time for this matter to be concluded. As a general rule, however, a challenge day can be a good time to ease off and not press forward on important issues. It is a good day to avoid any situations that may easily lead to conflicts.

Mystery and surprise days, I have found, are just that. I have received both **very good and not so good surprises** on those days. I feel that it is best to be relaxed and to flow with whatever happens.

It is good to keep a journal or diary and write down your experiences of each type of day for you. After a while you will see how the empowering, challenging, nurturing and surprise days affect you. Examine your experience of the day as it relates to your day sign, number and direction.

Also keep in mind the ruler of the week and how you relate to the ruler of the week. The correlation between the direction of your day sign and the way your day unfolds, during each new Mayan week, will validate and strengthen your appreciation of the system of Mayan astrology. This will help you to understand how the energy of the galactic center affects you. As you look back at how you used the day, you will come to find the way for interacting with challenge, mystery and support days that work for you. The more you think about and relate to the Mayan astrology, the stronger its help will be in your life.

This will give you even more validation that you are attuned to the Tzolkin.

In the original Mayan Calendar and Conversion Codex, there was no mention of the Mayan week and how to utilize that influence. In this book, the third level of connection to the Tzolkin comes with the acknowledgement of the Mayan week.

The first day of each new week sets the tone, or influences the rest of the day signs in the week. The influence of the present week is a bit different then the influence of the Mayan week into which you are born. The current Mayan week will be expressed in broader ways and many different areas of life. This means that if you are in a Monkey week, it may be a week that is filled with a lot of activity, creativity and movement. All the other days pay homage, so to speak, to the ruler of the week.

With the following information, you will get an impression of the general influence of the day sign of the week. I also make suggestions on how you might use the influence of the week, based upon the direction of your day sign. I will refer to the day signs by their direction, **East** (red), **West** (blue), **North** (white) and **South** (yellow) instead of their color.

For instance, it is good to take trips on weeks that are ruled by Dog and Deer, as both these day signs like to travel, hunt and generally move around a lot. It is good to start projects on Eagle, Crocodile and Serpent weeks. On an Eagle week, you can see the full potential of a project. Crocodile and Serpent weeks have the primal energy of creation moving through them. On weeks that are ruled by Star and Sun, it is good to be mindful that one may be inclined to go to excess in food and drink. Both these day signs are known for overindulgence. If you feel burned out and want to regenerate and regroup, you may want to do that on a Jaguar or Night week. Both these day signs carry the energy of renewal. A Transformer week is a good week to get married or start a business. The day sign Transformer represents stability and connection to the fertility and riches of the earth. As you can see, if you pay attention to the energy of the week, it can be very useful.

As you begin to understand the essence that each day sign brings to their particular week, that comes every 9 months, then you can make good use of the week for yourself. The following are suggestions on how to use each week. Whether it is a empowering, challenging, supportive or surprise week will depend on your day sign.

ONE CROCODILE

This week starts a new Tzolkin round, which means that the cycle of 260 days starts over on One Crocodile. During this 13 day period, there may be issues with family, security and education. The whole week brings good fortune and good financial outcomes. There may be some work needed to bring this about. Efforts will be well rewarded. It is a good time to start projects.

If your day sign is ruled by the **East** (red), then it is an empowering time for you to deal with these issues. If your day sign is ruled by the **West** (blue), then it is not a good time to press for these issues. If your day sign is ruled by the **North** (white) then you can be successful and lucky this week. For the **South** (yellow) born it might be a good idea not to initiate big changes in these areas of life. This week is a mystery/surprise week for you. If an event of this nature comes up by itself, then it is beneficial to address it.

ONE JAGUAR

During this period it is good to go within, and get in touch with your feelings. This can be a good time to make money or start relationships. If your day sign is **North**, you will find that it is a good time for starting new jobs or new projects that involve money. It is also a good time for those with North day signs to process some traumas from the past.

If your day sign is **South**, you may want to avoid emotional cleansing. It is not a good time to take on challenges with your finances or relationships.

Those who have day signs that are from the **East** will find this a good time for improving money situations and tense emotional situations in your life.

Those born under the **West** day signs will find that mysteries that have puzzled you for some time about relationships or finances may be solved or have light shed upon them.

ONE DEER

During this week you may feel a conflict between leaving behind a situation and staying to work out problems. It is a time when people are more sensitive to others and seek peaceful and tranquil solutions to personal interactions. It is also a time for expressing creativity and your love of what inspires you. It is also a good time to be out in nature or take a trip.

If you are born under a **West** day sign, then this is an empowering week for you to interact with others. If you are born into an **East** day sign, then it is best to leave problem solving in regard to group situations for another time. For those with a **South** day sign, you would find that expressing your creativity and feelings will be met with acceptance and support. It is a surprise week for those with **North** day signs. The general rule here is that if issues of this nature come up, then it is good to address them.

ONE SUN

During this thirteen day period, it is a time of getting out before people and expressing yourself. It is a good time for buying new clothes; furniture or housing. It can also be a time of extravagance, so you need to keep the spending in check. It might be time to be involved in creative activities. This is a week to connect with or heal feelings about people in your past. It could be good to visit graves of the departed or try to mentally commune with them.

For those born into **South** day signs, this can be a great time to express yourself. You can use this energy to get a new job, a raise, or start an artistic project. Your personal power is strong and expressive. For those born into **North** day signs, it is best to wait for another week to go shopping or look for a new job. This is a challenge week for you. Those with **West** day signs will get support in expressing their creativity and new directions. This is a supportive week for the blue born. The **East** day signs are in for surprises. They may be put in a situation to discover more about their talents or their heritage.

ONE REED

This thirteen day period is a great time for settling law suits, divorces, and setting new policies. It is an opportune time to air your opinions or ask for a raise. For the **East** day signs it is a time when you can make yourself heard to those who usually tune you out. The **North** day signs do well this week, as their opinions will find favor with their audience. It is surprise week for the **South** day signs. You may be called upon to speak your mind about a matter that has come to light. That which had been suppressed or hidden will now be revealed. For the **West** day signs, it may be a challenging time to speak your mind. You will find it healing, however, if you are called to do so.

ONE TRANSFORMER

This week is a powerful time for community activities. It is good to do business deals during this week. Marriage in a Transformer week assures a strong and prosperous union. It is a good time for social gatherings and networking.

For the **North** day signs, a Transformer week can be used to bring about major changes in business and family life. You will be heard and you will find success. For the **South** day signs, it is a time when thinking of the group instead of you could be a strengthening experience. This is your challenge week. The **East** day signs will have assistance in making changes for their family or other important groups. It is a supportive week for you. The **West** day signs are in for surprises this week. They may receive gifts or find that their bills are higher than expected. On a mystery/surprise week, anything can happen!

ONE STORM

As you can imagine, this can be a tumultuous week. The Storm influence of this week can bring cleansing and clearing or turbulence and many ups and downs. This week is a good time for going within and seeing what aspects of your shadow self are open now for healing. It is a good week to release addictions or start to learn some spiritual teachings. Your creativity can also be stimulated this week.

For the **West** day signs it is a time of power, when you can manifest your dreams. For the **East** day signs, it is a time for clearing and releasing. You will be challenged to look at what is within and allow what is not serving you to be washed away. The **South** day signs have a supportive week where they will go through these changes in a gentle, peaceful way. It is a good time to start projects that stimulate your creativity and connection to the sub conscious. It is a surprise week for the **North** day signs. People may unexpectedly come back into your life and bring turbulence with their presence.

ONE ROAD

As the energy continues from Storm to Road, we can see this week also has the focus of healing on the physical and emotional levels. A Road week can help you settle differences with friends and family. You will be clear on what you are feeling and how to express it simply during a Road week. It is also a good week for manifesting abundance. It is a good time for women to look at healing and releasing past traumas. It is a opportune for women to remedy any unresolved issues with other women.

For the **South** day signs, this is a time when situations that need healing can bring about magnificent transformations. It is a time to say what needs to be said. Don't keep your feelings bottled up. This can have a very nurturing conclusion when all is expressed and accepted. The **North** day signs will experience challenges in these areas. They may find it necessary to acknowledge physical or emotional situations that need to be healed. It may be hard to face these things, but they will be handled effectively during this time. For the **West** day signs this is a time when these areas of life can be healed in a very nurturing and peaceful way. Those born under an **East** day sign may have unexpected events occur that will bring healing when you have not even sought it out.

ONE SERPENT

During this week your instincts will serve you well. You will be able to take a stand on issues that have been eating away at you. The warrior energy within you can come to the surface now and be put into action. It is also a good week to do physical activity such as dancing or hiking.

The **East** day signs are at the height of their potential this week. You can break through barriers that you have not been able to break through before. The **West** day signs need to keep their emotions under control. An explosive outburst could resolve a situation, but it will not happen in a fun way. For the **North** day signs it is a time for you to stand up for yourself. The Serpent week will energize your warrior within to help you resolve emotional situations. Resolution will be easy and peaceful. **South** day signs may be confronted with situations that will call for them to stand up for themselves and dish out some touch love. They may be surprised at their emotional strength and the ability to follow through with this confrontation that can lead to a beneficial outcome.

ONE FLINT

During this week there will be a need for leadership that will come into your life. It is a time when you may have to make some decisions about your life calling. You may need to cut out some people or situations from your life. It is advantageous to take action at this time. It is a time when you may see that you are more competent then you had imagined. Communication will be effective this week.

It is a time when the **North** day signs can rise to leadership positions or simply lead the way for others to bring about their own decisions and changes. For the **South** day signs, this can be a challenging time when the need to make tough choices will be forced upon you .For the **East** day signs there will be a lot of help and diplomacy coming to you to help you take charge of situations that have gotten out of control. Those born under the **West** day signs will have unexpected demands put upon them. These day signs may be called into action to be competent and take charge before chaos takes over.

ONE MONKEY

During this week, it is time to have some fun and get creative! The monkey energy is very playful and mischievous, so don't take life too seriously! Those born under the **West** day signs will have an opportunity to get a great deal of attention. It is an excellent time for teaching, sales presentations and performances. The blue day signs will be able to shine this week. If you want be noticed by your boss or even a new love interest, then now is the time to go for the gusto! If the creative urge hits at this time, follow it for it will lead to positive experiences.

The **East** day signs may be in the spotlight but may not enjoy the experience. It is your challenge week. If you can take a situation lightly and not feel weighted down, this can turn into a pleasant time of helpful encounters. The **North** day signs may also find themselves unexpectedly becoming the center of attention. The white day signs will also find that their creativity is stimulated at this time. Even though the situation may be unanticipated, it can turn out well. The **South** day signs will enjoy being the center of attention and find that their creativity will flow easily. Starting creative projects this week is good for the southern day signs

ONE SEED

This week can bring out the sensual side of every day sign. It is a social week. Networking and other productive social interactions can have long reaching effects during this week. If you have the desire to expand promotion of your business, this is also a good week to get involved in the energy of this week. This week is considered to a lucky week by the Maya.

South day signs can really shine this week. You business ventures can prosper this week without much effort. Feel free to express your uniqueness. The **North** day signs will have to work hard to take advantage of the benefits that this week has to offer. It is your challenge week. They can enhance their financial situation, but only if they are willing to put in the required effort. The **West** day signs should have an easy, supported time in achieving their goals and could get lucky in many areas of life. They will find that even precarious situations will work out well. Good luck may also bless the **East** day signs, but in much unexpected ways. It could be good luck at the lottery for the red day signs this week!

ONE EARTH

This is a good week to get in touch with the mind and emotions. Being out in nature this week will not only revitalize you, but also brings emotional strength and personal growth. It is a good week to look at your past ideas that you want to manifest. Practical ways to birth your goals may come to you this week. It is also a good time to forgive others as well as yourself.

This is a perfect week for those born under the **East** day signs to go camping. You may find that you have the time and energy to tackle domestic problems like a leaky roof or cleaning out the spare bedroom. For the **West** day signs, it may be good to leave the redecorating for another week. Don't take your thoughts too seriously. You may find that you are having conflicts that need to be handled with people this week that revolve around a point of view. The **South** day signs may find themselves taking an unexpected trip to the country. Do not try to get others to see your side of the story unless you are confronted and need to make your stand clear. The **North** day signs will find this week very active mentally and they will find most interactions easy and flowing.

ONE DOG

This can be a very fun, light hearted week. It is a good time to travel and socialize. During a Dog week, you will be able to strengthen your bonds of loyalty to those you care about. It is also a good time for romance and sexuality.

The **North** day signs will enjoy themselves this week. They will see old friends and renew their connections. The northern day signs will also find that it is a good time to meet someone new or fortify an existing relationship .For the **South** day signs, it is not an opportune time to travel or be away from the ones you love. Don't risk socializing if it will create tension and feelings of disloyalty in existing relationships. The **East** day signs will have a lot of fun this week. You will enjoy the company of the people in your social circle and find that help in areas where you may be lacking will come through this week. The **West** day signs could get lucky unexpectedly this week. You may suddenly go on a romantic holiday or see friends that you haven't thought about in years. You might be socializing more then you thought!

ONE NIGHT

After all of the socializing of the last thirteen days, the reclusive energy of the Night day sign may be a welcome change. This is a time when one can retreat to their cave. The connection to the subconscious is very strong during this week. It can be a good time to deal with financial and security matters .Unfortunately, it is a time when spying and theft may prevail. Secrets that like to hide in the darkness may be revealed.

The **West** day signs can do very well with practical matters this week. It is a good time to take another look at finances and investments to make sure that everything is on track. It can be a strengthening time for **East** day signs. This is your challenge week, so you may be confronted with facing some tough financial or security issues. I know you don't want to deal with this, but facing it now will save you a lot of problems. The **South** day signs will have an easier time of it this week. They may find help in dealing with some financial or security issues. It could also be a time when hidden money or other important information will come to your awareness. The **North** day signs really need to be alert this week. You could get an unexpected inheritance or some unexpected bills. You may suddenly find out about some long held family secrets that may bring a lot of healing and understanding to all concerned.

ONE WISDOM

If you found a hidden mess or predicament during the last Mayan week, you will have the fortitude to clean it up or release it this week. The day sign Wisdom is able to clear or purify any unpleasant or limiting situations in your life. It is also a good time to think about forgiveness and releasing any unnecessary emotions and thoughts from your energy field.

The **South** day signs will see this week as an opportunity to do some physical cleansing and clearing .Fasting, sound healing or other activities that clear out the energy fields of the body will be helpful for the yellow day signs. The **North** day signs may want to purge their system of negative or unproductive thoughts and ideas. It is a challenge week for you, so this may happen whether you are seeking it or not. The unexpected need for purification may come upon the **East** day signs. This is your surprise week. It is a good time to release projects that are not finished and never will be. Handling these situations during this week can free your energy up for more creative and financially lucrative situations for the week to come when new projects will prosper. The **West** day signs will have an easier time of releasing what no longer serves them. They may even get support from loving friends and family with these issues this week.

ONE OFFERING

The energy governing this week can bring powerful emotional and creative expression or unpleasant outbursts. It is also a time when intuition is strong; you may be able to solve problems that have been bothering you for a long time. Addictions and other vices may be magnified during this week.

The **East** day signs will be feeling the Offering energy very strongly. They will find that expressing themselves this week can be beneficial. Follow your inner guidance this week, and it can have a very positive outcome for you. The **North** day signs, who could often benefit from emotional expression, will find themselves supported as they express their feelings. The white day signs could use a little passion in their lives! The **West** day signs will need to keep their emotions in check this week. It is your challenge week, so you may find anger and other painful feelings welling up this week. Take some deep breaths and try to express yourself in a positive way. Anything can happen for the **South** day signs this week. If a situation comes to your attention that angers you, try exercising or some other physical activity to help you get through these unexpected experiences.

ONE WIND

As you can guess, this is a very good week to communicate and to travel. The Wind energy can also be a bit fickle and flighty. Wind people are known for their angry tempers, so keep that in mind this week. You may have some interactions that could bring an angry wind out in you.

For the **North** day signs, this is a very productive week. The white day signs are in their element. Discussions, letters, surfing the internet can bring you what you need or desire this week. Traveling is also good now. The **East** day signs will also have a pleasant time this week. They will get very supportive communications. Even if you are too busy to really act on them this week, for the Wind day sign does bring a lot of movement into our lives, you can make some progress where communication is needed. The **South** day signs will be facing some communication challenges this week. Even the yellow day signs, that are not very verbal, will be put into a position to speak their mind. The yellow day signs can do well in business this week that involves precise communications. For the **West** day signs, this week will probably bring the need to communicate in ways that are not expected. Some unexpected travel or business presentations may be in store for you this week.

ONE EAGLE

During this week, it is good to make an effort to see the big picture of your life. Look at some long range planning for your future. It is also a time to pay attention to the details that you might not have been able to attend to during the busy Wind week. Eagle has the ability to see the forest and the trees.

It is a power week for the **West** day signs. As with the other western day signs, you can use this week to soar through their sub conscious and see what is lurking there. The western day signs are often intuitive, because they are at home in the underworld, where the sub conscious resides .The **South** day signs will find that they are able to make some long range plans this week that they will be able to carry out in the weeks and years to come. It is good for the earth bound yellow day signs to seek a higher purpose and the ways to manifest it. Those born under the **East** day signs are going to be having some challenges seeing the big picture. Try not to get bogged down in your emotions and look to expand your horizons. The **North** day signs will be getting some surprises when they examine their long range plans. There may be changes about their goals that they did not expect or plan for.

ONE STAR

This week can bring some confrontations and also some debauchery. The Star day sign is known for both. It is a good time to debate anything you are not happy about so that others can see your perspective. The Star week can bring out the fighter and the competitor in you. Keep this in mind when you are sharing your ideas.

The **South** day signs are motivated to express themselves this week. You will feel powerful, but keep what you are saying in perspective. If you do, you can win your debate! The **North** day signs may have a hard time standing up for themselves this week. Do not push to win important issues this week unless you are challenged to do so .Don't suppress what you have to say with alcohol or other addictive behaviors. The **West** day signs will not have to talk loud to be heard this week. Those that they need to convince will be open to listen, understand their side of the situation and make compromises. The **East** day signs may be surprised to find themselves in situations where they are forced to speak up and deal with a dilemma. Don't take it personally, just be strong and let your truth be known.

Your birthday week is the most powerful week of the Tzolkin round that comes every 9 months.

STEP THREE: CEREMONY TO WELCOME THE MAYAN WEEK

If you wish to go even further with integrating the energy of the source of all life, the Hu Nab Ku, into your life, you may want to do ceremony to welcome each new week of the Tzolkin. The Kiche' Maya, in the highlands of Guatemala, still do a simple ceremony every thirteen days to welcome and connect to the new Mayan Week. Doing the ceremony each 13 days will attune you to the energy of the ancient Maya and the living Maya that are doing this ceremony on the same day.

If you wish to do this step and honor the new Mayan Week, you will want to set up an altar for your ceremony. The traditional Mayan altar is very personal. It is usually set up in one corner of a room. The altar is put to the side so that it does not interfere with the rest of the daily life of the inhabitants of a usually crowded, one room, Mayan home. If you have a room that you can devote to ceremony, then have the altar against a wall in the center of the room. The furniture that you use for the altar should be covered with a cloth. The most important articles on the altar are Copal and candles. The candles can be any color. It is nice to use candles that are the color of the direction of the day sign of the Mayan week. The Copal can usually be purchased at any New Age bookstore or ordered on line. Copal cannot be lighted directly. You have to put it on a piece of burning charcoal that you can also get at New Age stores. Once the charcoal is red and glowing, you can sprinkle the little chunks of Copal on it. The Copal will start to smolder and give off a white, sweet smelling smoke.

Next you want to have flowers or a plant on the altar. You should also have pictures of departed loved ones, ascended masters, angels, or other spiritual beings. I like to put a little dish of white rum on my altar. Rum is used as an offering and is included in many types of Mayan ceremonies. Anything that represents spiritual energy for you is good to have on your altar. Other items to put on your altar may include tobacco, sugar and Rosemary. A live Rosemary plant is very good.

The ceremony should start at dawn, or as close to dawn as you can make it. I like to wear clothes that are the color of the direction that I am honoring. Light the charcoal and candles. Wait until the charcoal is ready and then put the Copal upon it. Once the Copal is smoldering with the white smoke, you are ready to start your ceremony.

Start off the ceremony with an energetic prayer to the day sign of the week. By this time you will have an understanding of the basic natures of all the day signs.

First, say something you know about the nature of the day sign.
" Oh, Day Sign Ajmak(or Wisdom)! I welcome you as the ruler of this new week. I ask that you help me with purifying my life and releasing what does not serve me."

If Wisdom is an **empowering day sign for you**, give thanks for empowerment in areas of your life that are in need. If it is a **challenge** day sign for you, ask for the resolution of conflicts and gentle lessons. If it is a **mystery** connection for you, say that you are thankful for all the gifts that come. If it is a **supportive** new week for you, give thanks for the nurturing that the week will bring you.

Next, you can set your intention for what you wish to accomplish for the new week. I like to write down my intentions for the week that I want to achieve. After I have made my prayer, I light the paper and let it burn alongside the Copal.

After saying the prayers and putting some more Copal on the charcoal, I sit down in front of the altar and let myself drift into a very deep, meditative state. The energy that I feel when I do this is different than what I feel when I am meditating or just sitting quietly with my eyes closed.

I have to say that I am connecting to a unique energy during the ceremony. Sometimes I have interested people join me for the ceremony. One person said that they saw, with their eyes closed, an old Mayan man and woman sit down amongst us. I have found orbs in pictures that I have taken near my altar. I have also received verbal messages. The ceremony to welcome the Mayan week can be very potent. You will be amazed at what you may experience at your personal ceremony.

After I have done my ceremony, I do the Mayan Day Keeper oracle..

WESTERN AND MAYAN ASTROLOGY WORK TOGETHER.

When studying a new astrology system, such as Vedic astrology, a person may feel a conflict of loyalty to one system over the other. Many feel that they must drop one system to fully embrace the other. With Mayan astrology there is no such conflict. Western and Mayan astrology work together because the **Western system focuses on the planets in our solar system** and **Mayan astrology focuses on the energy that comes from the center of our galaxy.** When you understand who you are in each system, you will have a complete picture of influence of the planets in the solar system and the light energy from the Milky Way.

The Western astrology system has definitions of personality as does the Mayan. These personality definitions are very accurate, or Western astrology would not have the popularity that it does.

I find the most interesting facet of Western astrology to be the transits. The transits show how the movements of the outer planets, Jupiter, Saturn, Uranus, Neptune and Pluto affect the planets at your time of birth, in your natal chart. The planets at the time of birth create an imprint upon each individual. When the outer planets that move slowly around the sun create an aspect or connection to your planets at birth, then you experience an influence of the transit in your life. Each of the outer planets brings a different influence to your life for a time period of a year or more. Some transits will impact a person's life for up to 4 years. Then the influence of the transit leaves your life. This can be very helpful in planning when to move, start a business or beginning a relationship. In my 20 some years sharing information about the transits with my astrology clients, I have found transits to be very accurate and helpful in planning major life transitions.

Mayan astrology is focused upon the individual and how their energy combines with the energy that comes from the galactic center each day. I have found the personality descriptions of Mayan astrology to be very astute. I have discovered that the Mayan astrology touches on parts of the personality that are not covered by Western astrology.

For example, I have a friend who is a Virgo in Western astrology. She has many of the Virgo traits such as attention to details, neatness, and concern with health. Yet, she is very out going, loves to be the center of attention at any gathering, is very artistic and works with her hands a great deal. When I found out that she was a Monkey, then these other aspects of her personality made sense to me. I think that when people discover their Mayan day sign, number and birth week influence, it will help them understand parts of themselves that are not covered by Western astrology.

Another helpful aspect of Mayan astrology is the emphasis on working with the energy of each day and week. The Mayan system encourages a person to look at their own energy and to be aware of how the present day will affect them. With Mayan astrology, a person will know that the energy from the galactic center will be harmonious, challenging, surprising or empowering each day. It gives a person a way to focus upon the present day and see how they may use this energy wisely.

The person who is following Mayan astrology will also be able to see how the present Mayan week will impact them. **When the energy of the day and the week are challenging, then the person knows not to push too hard during that day. If it is an empowering day and week for that person, it is good to ask for a raise, start a vacation or look into problems in a relationship.** The potentials for using the energy of each Mayan day and week successfully are limitless.

Using the knowledge of both systems will help a person honor their nature and use their energy to the fullest. When an individual is using their energy harmoniously and successfully throughout each day, it not only benefits them, but every life form in our galaxy.

REFRENCES

Andrews, Colin and Cynthia
    Complete Idiot's Guide to 2012, 2008
Barrios, Carlos
    The Book of Destiny, 2009
Barrios, Denise
    The Energies of the Day, 2010
Clow, Barbara Hand
    The Mayan Code, 2007
Gilbert, Adrian
    The Mayan Prophecies, 1995
Jenkins, John Major
    Maya Cosmogenesis 2012
Johnson, Kenneth
Jaguar Wisdom,1997
    Mayan Calendar Astrology: Mapping Your Inner
    Cosmos. 2011
Molesky-Poz, Jean
    Contemporary Maya Spirituality, 2006
Schele, Linda and David Freidel
    A Forest of Kings, 1990
Scofield, Bruce
    Day Signs, 1991,
    Signs of Time, 1994,
    How to Practice Mayan Astrology,
    2007
Tedlock, Barbara
    Time and the Highland Maya, 1982

Made in the USA
Las Vegas, NV
11 June 2022

50097582R00156